'The good ended happily and the bad ended unhappily. That
is what fiction means' – Miss Prism on her novel.

Oscar Wilde

CONTENTS

CONTENTS

Writers at Work

ACKNOWLEDGEMENTS

We would like to thank the publishers for permission to reproduce from the following:

Molloy, by Samuel Beckett, translated by Samuel Beckett and Patrick Bowles, John Calder, London, 1959. Copyright © Samuel Beckett 1950 and this translation 1955, 1959, 1966, 1971 and 1976, and Grove Weidenfeld, New York. Reproduced by permission of The Beckett Estate and the Calder Educational Trust, London and Grove Press, New York.

A Pale View of the Hills, by Kazuo Ishiguro, Faber and Faber, 1982.

The Government of the Tongue, by Seamus Heaney, Faber and Faber, 1988.

The Bookshop, by Penelope Fitzgerald, Duckworth, 1978.

Boris Pasternak, The Tragic Years 1930–60, by Evgeny Pasternak, Collins Harvill, 1990.

The Collected Poems of Wallace Stevens, Faber and Faber, 1985 and Alfred A. Knopf (USA and Canada).

Inferences on a Sabre, by Claudio Magris, translated from the Italian by Mark Thompson, Polygon, 1990.

Amalgamemnon, by Christine Brooke-Rose, Carcanet, 1984.

Transformation and Other Stories, by Franz Kafka, translated from the German by Malcolm Pasley, Penguin Books, 1992.

'A Hedge of Rosemary', by Elizabeth Jolley, from *Stories*, Fremantle Arts Centre Press, 1984.

'Two Men Running', by Elizabeth Jolley, from *Woman in a Lampshade*, Penguin Books Australia Ltd, 1983.

ACKNOWLEDGEMENTS

Alien Son, by Judah Waten, Sun Books, 1981.

'The Grasshopper's Burden', by William Goyen, copyright © 1985 by Doris Roberts and Charles William Goyen Trust. Reprinted by permission of Clarkson N. Potter, Inc., a division of Crown Publishers, Inc., US and Canada, and International Creative Management, Inc., UK.

Tolstoy, by Henri Troyat, translated from the French by N. Amphoux, Penguin Books 1987.

'Three in a Bed: Fiction, Morals and Politics', by Nadine Gordimer, is an adaptation of an essay which originally appeared in *The New Republic*. Copyright © Nadine Gordimer.

'My Turn', by Sara Paretsky, was originally published as 'Wild Women out of Control' in *Family Portraits: Remembrances of Twenty Celebrated Writers*, edited by Carolyn Anthony, published by Doubleday, a division of Bantam, Doubleday, Dell Publishing Group, Inc.

'Literary Landscapes', by Elizabeth Jolley, first appeared as 'Cloisters of Memory' in *Meanjin* 48, 3, University of Melbourne, Parkville, Victoria, 1989.

'The Devil Finds Work for Idle Hands', by John McGahern, is a development of an essay which appeared in the *Daily Telegraph* and *The New York Times*.

Writers at Work was first published in the *Guardian*.

The decorative initials used on the half-title pages throughout this book come from a set of woodcut initials by Jean Michel Papillon, Paris, 1760.

Every effort has been made to contact all copyright holders. The publishers will be pleased to make good any errors or omissions, brought to our attention, in future editions.

x

INTRODUCTION

Over and over the writers in this volume refer to 'the mystery' – that element in their work which is outside themselves but to which they aspire or submit, and the immense physical and intellectual labour that is involved in the harnessing of their creative skills and experience to this unquantifiable element through which, as Graham Swift says, the writer's imagination 'outreaches his personality'.

Most writers of fiction claim that the mystery cannot be explained (and should not be too closely investigated) but as the essays included here reveal, the compulsion to write, coupled with cunning, intelligence, endurance and a willingness to lay open oneself and pretty well lay down one's life, is all that is needed to engage with the mystery (if you are a story-teller, if you have a story to tell). Each writer here, in his and her own way, reveals a facet of that mystery.

The mystery, the magic, the gift is the very occasional reward that fiction writers get for keeping faith with an imagined ideal. The conscious appearance of the 'reward' in one's work is so rare as to be, as John McGahern puts it, 'like mirages in desert fables to encourage and torment the half-deluded traveller'.

But what of the rest? Mystery aside, accomplished fiction writers know what they are at and how they set about achieving their aims. John McGahern, again, says: 'Technique can certainly be learnt and only a fool would do without it' (although he adds, 'but technique for its own sake grows heartless'). Since the mystery is just that, then the whole of the author's skill lies in the mastery of the tools in his possession, which are no more than are in the

head and existence of every man and woman in the human race. What makes a writer commit his life to telling other people's stories? What is the mechanism that makes them come alive?

My earliest feelings, upon reading fiction, were not, 'I want to be a writer', but, 'How was that made?' As a child, I was not very interested in toys. I wanted to dismantle stories, to find out: what held them together, what was underneath, what made them work, where was trick and where was truth, why some stories made you feel better, why some put out leafy branches in one's own imagination. Anne Tyler once commented that when she was a child the stories she read in books seemed much more real than real life. That is exactly how I felt. In life, the moment of experience was always obscured by emotion. In stories, one could savour the incident and the emotion together – to hold and inspect occurrence and feeling, to analogously define sensation, to impose an order on event gave perspective, dimension and promise to life. When I grew up this curiosity did not go away, but got stronger, so that when I began my career as a journalist I spent most of my time interviewing writers, trying to find out how particular effects of style or structure were achieved. The novelist and short-story writer William Trevor helped me to understand the difference between long and short fiction forms. Jennifer Johnston advised me on how to balance the precarious budget of the fiction writer. 'Only budget on what you have earned by direct labour. All unexpected income – from repeats, film options, syndications, etc. must be designated as "fairy money" and used to buy treats.' Another eminent author helped me out when I was having trouble with my first novel which was too episodic. 'Try taking the last sentence of each chapter and making it the first sentence of the next,' he surprisingly suggested. Surprisingly often, it worked.

The treasure hunt continues here. The topics discussed include dialogue (Penelope Fitzgerald), plot (Patricia Highsmith), how to fudge the dull bits (Susan Hill), character (John Banville), editing (Fay Weldon). Graham Swift discusses the point of fiction and Malcolm Bradbury its relation to criticism. Rose Tremain de-

scribes the novelist's task of reimagining reality, Robertson Davies defends authors as performers and Nadine Gordimer, novelists as moral guardians. Marina Warner finds inspiration in a ragbag of curios and Hilary Mantel argues that ideas coaxed rather than bullied will grow naturally into a novel. Established writers will gain comfort from Jane Gardam's admission that 'every book is harder than the last' and from Brian Moore's assertion that: 'when a novel is finished the true novelist begins to forget what he has written.' These essays are also for all those people who are trying to write, who have not yet got the nerve to call themselves a writer, nor the time to commit themselves fully to what they love, nor the ear, as I had, of other tolerant and patient authors. To encourage these readers I have included some successful early novelists. I have also put in a short selection of interviews from a series, Writers at Work, which I wrote for the *Guardian*, to convey the curious servitude that is a writer's life and perhaps to discourage false vocations. The idea for the anthology came to me when I was lecturing at writers' workshops. I became aware of the need for some collective (and sometimes dissenting) voices on the subject of fiction writing, upon which isolated and insecure writers can try out their own voices. I also feel this volume is a timely introduction to the interior world of fiction in a period when literary theory has, perhaps, over-busied itself with the externals of the form.

Writing fiction is a paradox because all of it comes out of ourselves. There is nowhere else for it to come from. Yet when the characters of a novel have been established the fiction writer's task is to remove himself and his influence, and let the characters get on with their lives. This, more than anything, is the essence of this work – the investment and then the withdrawal of the fiction writer – the agony and the ego – although I think it should probably be the other way round.

This anthology does not claim to comprehensively cover the world of fiction, not even current fiction. There were many topics I wanted covered which the contributors did not wish to address.

There were many more novelists I wanted to include, but I failed to attract them, although I tried. Inevitably, it reflects the kinds of work that I like and try to emulate. Nonetheless, I have no hesitation in saying it is an inspiring collection, in the truest sense of the word. Each time I have read it I have found myself reaching for my notebook, some creaky mechanisms released, and the excitement, which is the whole point of writing fiction, temporarily restored. The intention of this book is not to teach people how to write. I would agree with the view of many fiction writers that creative writing, coming as it does out of one's own centre, cannot be imparted to another. I would, however, disagree completely that one ought not to advise and guide and share something of what one knows on the basis that there are already enough works of fiction in the world. This is simply not true. Writers have lost faith who do not believe that there are still more gifted but obscure story-tellers out there and that some need a wise or kind word, a renewal of conviction, a sense of solidarity to free them from their apprehensions. What has often struck me most is the loneliness of the writer – not the solitude, which is a blessing – but the self-doubt, the rejection, the small financial return, the boredom of being confined with a frequently narcoleptic set of characters. This volume is a helping hand from some of the most eminent living writers to all other writers who lack a constant network of support. It is the great and the good saying: 'This is where I fell (this is where I still fall), this is where I found a foothold, this is my belief, this is my talisman, this is my best tip – and this is what I saw when I dared to gaze into the gift, the burden, which comes from a part of myself that I have had to discover, and somewhere outside of myself that I do not know at all.'

The contributors to this anthology are among the leading fiction writers living today. They do not in general analyse their work. It is a painful and difficult (and some feel dangerous) thing to do. I have been astonished by their generosity and thank them for it.

THE FIRST MYSTERY

Rose Tremain

The imagination conjures gifts; what the ungrateful, unsentimental part of the mind has to do is to unwrap them, . . . see them for what they are and then alter them.

Rose Tremain is a novelist and short-story writer, whose novel, *Restoration*, won the *Sunday Express* Award and the Angel Award and was short-listed for the Booker Prize. Her sixth novel, *Sacred Country*, was recently published.

THE FIRST MYSTERY

On a rainy afternoon in August 1983, I lay down in a hotel bedroom in Bourges and had a waking dream.

I imagined a middle-aged man standing by a low stone wall, somewhere in the French countryside. He had thinning, sand-coloured hair. He appeared tired and melancholy. He looked up at the clear sky above him and saw an enormous bird circling there. He realized it was an eagle and his expression changed from sorrow to wonder. The eagle kept turning lower and lower. It landed on the wall right in front of the man and perched there, regarding him. Now, the man beamed. He felt violently happy. He understood that something miraculous had occurred.

This sequence of images, carrying in it the idea of sudden transformation or transcendence, was the fragile foundation of my novel *The Swimming Pool Season*. It was what I shall call the 'first mystery' of the book, the thing that will – or might – contain the essence of what that book is going to be, provided the significance of the mystery can be rightly interpreted. By 'rightly', I mean that the writer's task is to bring the 'first mystery' to earth, in order to extract from it a meaning that will serve the work.

The Bourges dream, containing as it does the miraculous thing that literally comes out of the sky, has been useful in helping me to understand one part of the process of novel writing – that part in which the imagination conjures images and the controlling authorial mind gives them context and meaning.

There exists, I believe, throughout the writing of a novel, a constant traffic of the mysterious or random towards an absolutely unmysterious and un-random place in the narrative. Thus, in

The Swimming Pool Season, the man/eagle mystery is decoded to provide me with the idea of a man (an Englishman) more or less defeated by life, living in exile in France, for whom something extraordinary has to happen to give him some sense of self-worth. The man becomes the protagonist of the novel, Larry Kendal, a builder of swimming pools. Late on in the book, he *does* see an eagle on a wall, but this isn't the 'something extraordinary' that starts a period of recovery from failed hopes. What actually happens is that Larry finds inspiration in a Byzantine cathedral for 'the most beautiful swimming pool of all'. The 'first mystery' is now unrecognizable. Yet, without it there would have been no book. Or at least, not *that* book.

In *Restoration*, my 'first mystery' was a white room in a tower, filled with light. I saw a large man, wearing gaudy clothes, standing in it and looking out. The man quite soon became my seventeenth-century physician and fool, Robert Merivel, but for a long time, until I understood it correctly, I thought the white room might be the location for the beginning of the story. It wasn't until I had abandoned the room altogether that I saw that it was in fact the place where the whole thing *ends*, the point towards which Merivel's journey drives and which serves also as a metaphor for Merivel's mind itself, symbolizing his late acquisition of wisdom.

In this novel, other random or coded images were: a Quaker lying on a hard bed, holding a china soup-ladle; a woman's voice, singing, heard through a closed door; mist coming off the Thames in a summer dawn. They had no meaning and belonged nowhere. Significance and context had to be found for them. Thus, the Quaker became the moral and intensely inward character, Pearce; the woman singing became Celia, the King's inaccessible mistress and the pivot on which the whole plot turns; the mist lifts to reveal the jewelled person of the King sculling downstream to Kew, and it is this immensely important moment that reawakens in Merivel his old longing to be returned to the King's favour. So – on and on – the imagination conjures gifts; what the ungrateful,

unsentimental part of the mind has to do is to unwrap them, find fault with them, see them for what they are and then alter them.

But in novel writing, the trafficking is not all in one direction. Just as the random must find its own essentiality, so – in the opposite direction – the factual or experiential has to find its own mysteriousness. By this I mean that all the research done for a novel – all the studying and reading, all the social fieldwork, all the location visiting, all the garnering of what is or what has been – must be reimagined before it can find a place in the text. It must rise into the orbit of the anarchic, gift-conjuring, unknowing part of the novelist's mind before it can acquire its own truth for the work in question.

Graham Greene, when asked by a journalist how he would make use of an important experience he'd had in South East Asia, replied: 'It's yours to remember and mine to forget.' He was talking about the novelist's task of reimagining reality. Reimagining implies some measure of forgetting. The actual or factual has to lose definition, become fluid, before the imagination can begin its task of reconstruction. Data transferred straight from the research area to the book will simply remain data. It will be imaginatively inert.

My new novel, *Sacred Country*, opens in the year 1952, at the moment when King George VI is buried and the new Elizabethan age begins. I wanted to use this moment in history, pinpoint it, fix it as a beginning. On the day of the King's funeral, there was a two-minute silence at two o'clock, to be observed by everyone everywhere in Britain, and I decided to begin the novel there, in that silence. But the task was to give the silence powerful meaning for my central characters and also – because this is an opening section – to make thematic sense of it. At first, this felt like an immensely difficult task.

The imaginative solutions I found are these: the silence contains the first epiphany of my protagonist, Mary Ward, the moment in childhood when she realizes she isn't really a girl at all, but a boy; the silence lasts longer than the designated two minutes for the

Ward family (Mary's father's watch is damaged and he's unable to time the silence accurately) and so brings in the idea that these lives are somehow unsynchronized with the mainstream of history.

For *Sacred Country*, alone among the six novels I've written, there does not seem to be any 'first mystery'. There is just the complex idea of the unsynchronized life and around that fixed edifice a lot of unruly traffic has to pass and re-pass in opposite directions. But, looking back now at the shape of the novel, I am beginning to wonder whether there isn't something called a 'last mystery', which may only become clear after all sound of traffic has ceased.

ANGELS AND DAEMONS –
THE ANATOMY OF A NOVEL

Jane Gardam

Every novelist knows the urge to burst out with what they're up to and learns that only a fool does so. This isn't because ideas get stolen (though they do) but because the idea for a novel, when dropped into conversation, sounds so banal . . . 'A novel about a pop group? *Really*?' 'A novel about a group of ageing men? In Wales? . . .' 'A novel about biting into a little cake? Three volumes of it? Taking about a year to read? . . .'

Jane Gardam, novelist and short-story writer, has written for children as well as adults. She has won a number of literary prizes including the David Higham Award and the Winifred Holtby Memorial Prize. Her most recent novel, *Queen of the Tambourine*, was awarded the Whitbread Prize and an earlier novel, *God on the Rocks*, was short-listed for the Booker Prize.

ANGELS AND DAEMONS –
THE ANATOMY OF A NOVEL

It is impossible to say when a novel begins its life or when it is complete. It has a subterranean existence of its own before it reaches the paper, perhaps before it reaches the writer, and again after it has gone on its travels. 'Did I write that?' you ask years later. 'How embarrassingly bad.' 'Did I write that? How surprisingly good.' Once it is published a novel is no longer your own. Like your child (and sometimes you don't like your child) it leaves you to reveal new things about itself to new people. If its characters (and that's what a novel is about, characters: the plot must look after itself except in thrillers and perhaps even then) are not contestable, arguable, differently interpreted by different readers, then the book has not been worth good money.

This is the novel's after-life. Its pre-natal life is as odd. Where on earth – if on earth – does a novel come from? All we can be sure of is that it comes from the deep somewhere and is an attempt to put things in some sort of shape. That's to say, to put people in some sort of shape. 'Story-telling,' says Graham Swift, 'is an instinct to come to terms with mystery, chaos, mess.'

This cannot be done all at once. Most novels of any weight at all seem to have been inspired by ideas long kept silent. The keeping silent seems to me to be important. Every novelist knows the urge to burst out with what they're up to and learns that only a fool does so. This isn't because ideas get stolen (though they do) but because the idea for a novel, when dropped into conversation, sounds so banal. Like other people's wallpaper. You think, 'Oh dear – surely not!' We all know the blank look of the most

percipient friend or critic. 'A novel about a pop group? *Really*?' 'A novel about a group of ageing men? In Wales? Is that quite your area?' 'A novel about biting into a little cake? Three volumes of it? Taking about a year to read? About the fall of angels and the meaning of God and the imagination? Oh really, Marcel! Oh really, Salman!'

We have to make the choice alone and for ourselves and keep it to ourselves. In Art you keep most of your own counsel. You risk your damask cheek.

And a risk it is. The complexion of a novelist is seldom rosy (Paul Bailey once announced to a heavy-hearted audience of novelists at PEN that we have always been an ugly tribe). We are engaged in indoor activity, haemorrhoidal, prone to chilblains, poor of circulation. Nadine Gordimer has called it 'an obsessive, neurotic life', where we 'sit hour after hour, day after day, quite alone'. It is a life under stress, schizogenic. We are not engaged in the simple reportage of things. 'I don't go round looking for material from my life that will make a novel' – Graham Swift again – 'nor do I turn people whom I know into characters. Once I have invented characters I see things through their eyes.' Intense, draining, exhausting, solitary, anti-social, mad.

But very delightful. It's easy to forget this in all the welter about writers' blocks and anguish of expression. Alison Lurie thinks that among young novelists today there's too much talk about 'suffering'. I myself was sharply told to pull myself together by my publisher when I was moaning about the difficulties of writing with three children around the house. Look at E. Nesbit, I was told, at wonderful Mrs Gaskell. Look at the superb novelist Jennifer Johnston who has nine of them. A psychiatrist friend sorted me out about writer's block, too. 'Of course you have,' she said, 'you'd be no good if you hadn't. It's a clinical condition after completing a book. It's called tiredness. The mind has to restore itself. There are times when you physically *cannot* write – so no point worrying. Go out and dig a ditch.'

After all, nobody *has* to write a book. Nobody asked us to.

And have you ever met any writer who seriously would be anything else?

And as to wanting to be anything else, another mystery. Is there a sort of person who writes fiction? It's possible there may be. After all, it has just been discovered that there is a linguistic gene in the brain that can pass from generation to generation surviving all kinds of differences of education and experience; so what about a story-telling gene? Story-telling, like a facility for languages (and music and mathematics) does tend to run in families. Or is it tribal? Is the urge to tell stories based on ancient tribal culture? Why are there so many Yorkshire novelists? Why so many Indians? These are mysteries, too.

Even the story-tellers who haven't much time for the idea of mystery, the 'Method' writers who work from stacks of notes and drawers full of discs of painstakingly researched data, still have to explain their urge to produce fiction on the page. Why this form of communication rather than another? Books? Are we not being told that books are on the way out? Why do these often hard-nosed worldly people choose to live this way? Is it still the same mystery? Whoever the writer, wherever he or she comes from, finding the way in to the source of invention, the well in the forest, is always peculiar and appears – discs, notes or not – to be haphazard. To write, there are times when you must hang about. You must loiter and dream. It is like waiting for an Indian train or walking in the Cevennes. The trail is apt to be stumbled upon by accident when you're least looking for it, however many maps and blankets and flasks for the journey you've brought along. Yet another mystery.

And because it is a mystery I am wary of those who think all can be rationalized and made smooth by instruction. I am particularly wary of creative writing classes. I know they can sometimes be helpful. They can cosset and encourage, and some teachers can inspire and may be able to give help about publication and so on; and they can cheer up the lonely souls (especially in the coffee breaks) but they cannot teach the spirit of light that wakes the

imagination – kick-starts it like an electric charge. This blast of pleasure has to happen of itself. It is given. If it doesn't happen – well, there are other kinds of writing you can do.

Iris Murdoch calls this electric charge her daemon. Our daemon is a creature we have no control over and it may arrive or desert us at any time.

But having been visited by the daemon, life – and our novel – still does not go rationally along. There is no immediate compulsion as a rule to do anything about it. Like love, if it is the real thing there is often no sense of urgency. The supreme delight is recognition and for a time can exist in holding hands. We're like bulbs in winter waiting for the weather. Some say that Dickens first saw the immortal name of Pickwick above a shop in the Strand when he was bowling along on the top of a bus; others say that Pickwick was a man in charge of a coaching business somewhere in Kent near Dickens's old home. Whichever is true – maybe both are true – Pickwick lived in Dickens's notebooks for over a year and perhaps (if it was Kent) for very much longer before someone asked for a set of stories about 'some members of a sporting club'. Pickwick then stood forth, booted and buttoned and in splendid voice, surrounded by his pals, and London was at his feet within the month.

And Trollope, who we never stop hearing wrote instantaneous fiction by the metre, is really using (if you read his biography) mile upon mile of experience from his provincial childhood and young manhood. It's interesting how the so-called first social-consciousness novels of the nineteenth century – the 1840s novels, the great age – are rooted and grounded so often in the authors' childhoods of thirty or so years before.

There is no hurry – unless we're dying. Sufficient to know that we are fictionally cast. It is a distinction, even if it's painful now and then. Gerard Manley Hopkins attached a sea-anemone to his forehead when he was young because it was so beautiful – and then he squawked because of the marks it made.

With me the idea for a novel has always arrived with an image,

which has often been the same one, of a child walking alone on a beach. This has seldom turned out to be the first scene in the book. Sometimes it hasn't even turned up in the book at all in the end, or only heavily disguised. I was rather sensitive about it at one time and hoped it wouldn't be noticed for I felt I must be a very limited writer. I only cheered up – and considerably – when I read somewhere that Hardy begins almost every one of his novels with the figure of someone walking on a lonely road. (Do not despise your instincts like some awful parents affect to despise their children: 'My dear – they're frightful! Sometimes I think they are *retarded*!' This is cruel and shallow and not modest at all.)

My beach is always full of light. The light is the seaside of my childhood and it is not surprising for the beaches of the north-east coast are famous. They are the wonderful five miles of white sands that so excited Carroll. He wrote *The Walrus and the Carpenter* about them on an Oxford vacation there. They are also the sands of the less poetic but equally passionate Gertrude Bell, the Arabian explorer. She used to ride there as a child on her donkey and one supposes they were where she learned to think of the desert.

I'm not sure my fascination for the sands was not put there by my mother who had also played on them as a child and one day walked all alone as far as the distant breakwater at South Shields. Suddenly she had grown frightened. There was nothing frightening to be seen but she was filled with terror. Then, out of the sand-hills walked a sandy dog who politely escorted her all the way home. She believed that this dog had been sent from God to protect her. This was the first story I think I ever heard.

When I was five I wandered off on the sands in the same way and returned after hours to general pandemonium. They'd told me to go off and play as I was under their feet, so I had done so. What shrieks! They were tearing their hair. I was smug as a cat.

My mother said, 'You must thank God that He looked after you,' but I don't think I did. I believe something happened to me on the beach that day, now quite buried. Nothing bad. There was

no other person in it. It was not Krishna appearing in his essential form. Yet some sort of freedom occurred. Something eternal.

Meeting God? I knew of course from my mother that nobody has ever met God but I didn't pay much attention to it because in fact I was always seeing Him or something or other to do with Him. The first time was on the prom, when I was six and we were out to see the Illuminations. Somehow I had become separated from my parents and I stood in the surge of the tall crowds in the dark. I remember thinking, I must seem very sure of myself, and turning for home, and there stood God, or one of His archangels, willowy and high above me and wearing a pale grey suit. He had a neat little silvery Vandyke beard. 'Are you lost?' he asked and I said 'Oh, no.' I frightened the maid when I walked into the kitchen alone – she was reading a magazine, her legs all over the table top and her knees showing. She flew out with me again to find my parents who were proceeding towards us from another direction, and then the whole lot of us got lost. I didn't say much about the archangel until somebody rather like him turned up in *Crusoe's Daughter*, forty years on.

The second time I encountered the Lord was on some waste ground beside the railway the same summer. He was down in the long grass picking dog-daisies and this time he was plump, his beard rounded, white and fluffy. He was crawling about with his fists full of daisies, like Nebuchadnezzar in Blake's picture but I didn't know that then.

Were they lucky escapes? They were lucky encounters, colour-plates I put away. Nebuchadnezzar emerged in 1978 as the mad painter in *God on the Rocks*.

My latest novel, *Queen of the Tambourine*, is the first without the sea in it. There is only a pond. The image this time occurred in Wimbledon, in the Worple Road, when outside the supermarket a good-looking, well-dressed woman – hair expensively cut, face beautifully painted – came careering past me with her mouth wide open and stretched taut. It was like a dark cave. She was silently screaming. Mad as a hare.

Nobody paid any attention. I said to a woman coming along behind, 'Did you see that?' and the woman said, grim and striding, 'Yes, I *did*!' Eliza Peabody and all her circle – all of whom the Americans would call her 'neighbourhood friends' were born in that instant – splash. Like rabbits.

Then they all went away, only emerging two years later, like Moses in the bulrushes, when they had seemed quite forgotten; and like Pharaoh's daughter I excitedly gathered them up.

This time it wasn't Wimbledon but France – a ghastly holiday in Burgundy, a dark, ice-cold spring and everything dripping, every hostelry full. We had at last found a sort of guesthouse, a mill, with a notice three feet high saying COMPLET but we went in and sat until at last the Madame let us have a room up a flight of stone steps that climbed a wall. A wild, sopping wisteria scattered icy drops on us as we went up. It later appeared on Eliza's honeymoon.

The stone room through the door at the top of the steps was wonderful and looked out across a vineyard. The little wet vines shone out black and knobbly, patent leather in the rain. Some geese tipped about under the window, talking and spooning things up in their beaks. It could not have been farther from the Worple Road.

I sat in the window-seat – ice-cold stone – wrapped in a blanket off the bed and a mat off the floor, reading Aldous Huxley. It was a story about a very old writer long thought dead. The literary world had given a party for him that night to celebrate his rediscovery. When at last the party was over the happy old man moved around his fungoid bed-sit in Chelsea singing an antique song from the music-halls, 'in a tiny voice like the voice of a gnat',

> For she's the Queen
> Of the Tambourine,
> The cymbals and
> The Bones.

The innocence, the beauty of it! I beamed on the geese and across

the vines, and there, standing among them was the mad suburban woman, the image of suffering, yearning for joy. The book followed.

It was more than a year later though that I actually began the writing of it. Maybe two years. They were not empty. I published a book of short stories, did a great deal of reviewing, judged a burdensome literary prize that destroyed a summer. My mother and then my father died within five weeks of each other. My first grandchild was born. My hitherto mostly dependable Catholic faith went suddenly numb. We idiotically moved out of London after thirty years, away from children, friends and work. The whole prism was shaken.

But the figure with the cave-mouth was still around, offstage the beat of the tambourine, not yet comprehensible but insidious. At last one day I sat down quickly and began.

The start was encouraging (I never changed a word of the first chapter which I wrote as three private letters) and soon I got down to the first true draft of the full book which took six weeks. It was Lent and old habits die hard. I had given up drink which wonderfully concentrates the mind. After Easter (and the blessed Tokay again) I got down to the harder work of deciding what I really was up to and for about three months I worked about four hours a day and often longer.

Every book is harder than the last and this one was very hard indeed because of all the literary criticism and analysis of literature I'd been doing for the past two or three years. I had changed, and my view of fiction had changed. I had begun to think about what fiction is and is not. I still believed that the most important thing about it is to entertain, but now 'entertaining' had become a much more serious thing, an 'entertaining novel' is much more fluid, healthier and wiser than the novel with a purpose, the novel that sets out to instruct. Entertainment takes in pure joy and pure agony too.

But it must never be ingratiating and the reader really has to look after himself. You must forget that the reader exists while

you are getting the book right. 'I love my characters, good and bad,' says Graham Swift again (he can't be quoted too often), 'but it's not as if I'm counsel for their defence and it's not as though I can prevent terrible things happening. In some ways writers have to be cruel.'

Fiction is not about harmony either. We are arranging, giving shape to chaos, but we are not creating harmony. Interestingly we are sometimes writing about happy endings (though there are of course no real endings) where they are correct. It would be as silly to cast out the idea of a happy ending *per se* as it would be to try to manufacture one. I love a happy ending but I'm not a fool.

And so, after the end of my first draft of this novel, I found myself in a fix. I was awash with theory and my story-telling faculty had left me. I sat longing for an easy talent – to be the sort of writer who could make a grid, a taxing, binding structure to hold all the random, chaotic ideas and frightening forces of my dear mad heroine together. No – not my mad heroine – my half-mad, half-sane heroine, the heroine whom I so wanted to fill with life. She was dead as a case history.

I began to spread myself about then, I invented a great many secondary characters. Then I got rid of the lot of them. (One day I killed off a whole train-load coming from Oxford. 'Away with you,' I said.) Next I took hold of Eliza and roughed her up. I took ten years off her age – reluctantly, because I'd been taken with Arnold Wesker's idea that 'a woman of sixty is a volcano', but I decided that a sixty-year-old volcano hanging yearningly over a young man's bed – which is what Eliza does – is not pleasing. Fifty is just all right. Sixty is kinky and there is nothing less interesting than a novel of an extended menopause. Or any menopause, come to that. But there was something wrong with the form of this novel. I decided – very bravely because it is unfashionable, almost antique – to do the book completely as letters: the epistolary novel publishers so hate.

Yet, would Eliza have written letters? Was she too mad for them? For good ones? And to whom would she have written? She

is cut off, shipwrecked. Aha! Suddenly, sweetly the plot began to emerge.

The letters would be to nobody. That's to say they would be to Eliza's fantasies – the mother she never had, the lover she never had, the perfect friend she never had, the beloved husband who has gone. Most of all they would be to the child she never had. All the recipients of these letters would be rolled up into one person (let's call her Joan), and Eliza would at last, tentatively, slowly, bravely, face what's been wrong with her: face her two terrible secrets. She would save herself. And all *by* herself. My mad, pathetic, bossy, suburban Eliza would become what Victorian novelists used to call 'fine'.

It was plain sailing then. I adored writing the letters. They were such a pack of lies. Eliza, of course, didn't tell the truth ever (although she often reports actual happenings) until the last letter. None was even posted until then.

But no letters tell the truth anyway. No fiction ever tells the truth. 'The best we can do' – Muriel Spark – 'is write words from which a kind of truth emerges.'

So I took my Eliza to the brink of the bin, holding someone's baby above a lake and dropping it in – then fishing it out. I never really was tempted to let her drown the child, though the critics despised me for my cowardice. Fiction is full of mad women drowning children and Eliza is not ordinary. She could not have done it. Calm, quiet, stronger and alas now rather dull – my heroine recovered, and left me. The book was over.

For maybe half a day I had great euphoria. I decided that I would go right back again to the beginning of it. I felt strong as a lion. I felt I could improve and improve. I could roll back on stage all that host of characters and add to them – give them each their story. I could open everything out into a great sea of subsidiary stories. A flood. My daemon reappeared however at this point. He coughed politely and said no. 'Enough is enough,' he said. 'We don't want any showing off. We don't want this "look, no hands" stuff. It's the tambourine, not a full philharmonia with organ and

trumpets. Let the girl be. She's on her own now.' Then he vanished.

Another image, please God, will follow along.

POSTSCRIPTIVE THERAPY

Graham Swift

A true writer's imagination is always bigger than he is, it outreaches his personality. Sometimes this can be felt palpably and thrillingly in the very act of writing, and perhaps it is for this infrequent but soaring sensation that writers, truly, write.

Graham Swift has written five novels including *Shuttlecock*, *The Sweet Shop Owner* and the internationally acclaimed *Waterland*, which was short-listed for the Booker Prize and has been filmed. His most recent novel is *Ever After*.

POSTSCRIPTIVE THERAPY

If I were asked what is the essence of story-telling, I would say it is a simple thing: the relating of something strange. Somewhere behind any work of fiction, long or short, is a voice quietly insisting, 'Isn't it strange? This life that we thought so familiar and straightforward, it isn't really so familiar and straightforward at all.' The novelist or short-story writer may employ more sophistication but, at bottom, he is doing nothing different from the man in the pub who begins, 'A funny thing happened to me . . .' or 'You won't believe this, but . . .' Be it amusing or heart-rending, a story begins with the recognition of the strange.

I try not to forget the man in the pub, that figure with his brimming urge to tell. A cursory scanning of my work will show that I favour the first person. One reason I do so is that I do not want simply to tell, out of the blue, a story. I want to show the pressure and need for its telling. To put it another way, I am as interested in the narrator as in the narrative. I want to explore the urgency of the relation between the two.

The realization that 'things are strange' may be exciting and exhilarating; it may also be deeply disturbing. My narrators are frequently people who have suffered or are undergoing some personal crisis. They have lost their hold on experience and their need to tell their story is driven by the desire to regain that hold. I have no doubt that one of the principal functions of story-telling is therapeutic: it is a way we have of dealing with those sometimes distressing questions, 'What happened to us?', 'What became of us?', 'How did we get to this?' I do not believe that stories can be prescriptive, that they can tell us in any direct way how to live,

23

but they can be positively, benignly 'postscriptive'. By recovering our lost or damaged pasts we also, simply, recover. We strengthen, we go on.

There is another reason why I use the first person. I want to be in the pub myself. I want to be there, at ground level, sharing his space, with the man at the bar. But I am not my narrators, my narrators are not me. Writers who choose the first person are perhaps particularly subjected to a common assumption that fiction is in some way really an autobiographical process – the writer's own direct experience is deliberately exploited or sublimated for the purposes of story-telling. This is a view I find dispiriting, not least because it is actually *against* fiction, it tries to reduce fiction to fact.

Deep down, of course, everything a writer writes must be of and from that writer's self – it is absolute and ineluctable self-expression. But this does not mean that its mainstay is the reworking of personal experience.

One often hears offered as indispensable advice to young writers: 'Write only about what you know – write from your experience.' I could not agree with anything less. My maxim would be: for God's sake write about what you *don't* know! For how else will you bring your *imagination* into play? How else will you *discover* or *explore* anything? And if you stick to your own experience as the only stock of your literary ventures, what happens when that stock – which must be limited, even if it *is* interesting to anybody else – runs out?

One of the fundamental aims of fiction is to enable us to enter, imaginatively, experiences *other* than our own. That is no small thing. The hardest task in the world, against which consciousness stacks insuperable obstacles, is to understand what it is like to be someone else, but upon that vital mental endeavour so many of our moral, social and political pretensions depend. Fiction, after all, serves the real world. No fancy theories are needed: it begins with strangeness, it takes us out of ourselves but back to ourselves. It offers compassion.

Readers of my novel *Waterland* have been surprised, even disappointed, to learn that I do not come from the Fens of East Anglia but from London. The surprise even merges with suspicion: surely I *must* come from there – if not, have I not perpetrated some sort of fraud? This reaction overlooks, or certainly underestimates, the imagination. Fiction is not fact, but it is not fraud. The imagination has the power of sheer, fictive invention but it also has the power to carry us to the truth, to make us arrive at knowledge we did not possess and may even have felt, taking an empirical view of our experience, we had no right to possess.

I confess I do not understand this power and I cannot explain it, but I have absolute faith in its existence. It is what for me constitutes the magic of writing and, I trust, the magic of reading. A true writer's imagination is always bigger than he is, it outreaches his personality. Sometimes this can be felt palpably and thrillingly in the very act of writing, and perhaps it is for this infrequent but soaring sensation that writers, truly, write. There may be days and days of labour, when the imagination is tethered and the writer is all too aware of the self and its lonely effort, but there are those rare days too, of revelation, of ecstasy, when the writer can do no more than acknowledge with gratitude and wonder: this thing is bigger than me.

RICH PICKINGS

Marina Warner

My Catholic girlhood taught me two disciplines that are invaluable, I think, for writing: the daily examination of conscience and the meditation on holy pictures.

Marina Warner is an author of major art and historical works as well as an accomplished novelist. Her third novel, *The Lost Father*, was short-listed for the Booker Prize. Her most recent novel is *Indigo* and she has a new collection of short stories, *The Mermaids in the Basement*.

RICH PICKINGS

For my last novel, I kept around me:

1 bottle bay rum
2 oyster shells (fitting together)
A photograph of Thomas Warner's tomb in the churchyard of
  Old Road, St Kitt's, West Indies
A postcard of a Dutch painting of a young Indian mother and her
  child in Surinam, 1641
A Greek vase showing Circe mixing something in a bowl for
  Odysseus
Dried sorrel vine
Flakes of crystals from the bed of a sulphur spring

The bay rum was for my father, who always used it, so that I
could summon him up before me just at a whiff; oysters act as the
book's key image, the female sex symbolized as a sea-creature,
which seemed right for a novel that explores *The Tempest*; the
painting by Albert Eckhout helped me imagine the life of the
islanders before the British changed everything (there aren't any
images from that time by the indigenous people themselves, so we
have to rely, with a pinch of salt, on representations by the
empire-builders); St Kitt's is the island which inspired the forested,
volcanic geography of the novel, where my ancestors settled as
early colonists in the mid seventeenth century. Shakespeare's
Sycorax, the silenced (dead) mother of Caliban, might have been
inspired by the Greek enchantress Circe, who could turn men into
beasts – I followed this line of imagery but tried to invert the
dread and disgust expressed by Prospero. The sorrel vine and the

crystals formed part of the pharmacopœia that my Sycorax uses in her various experiments in cooking and dyeing and healing, arts which she passes on to her adopted daughter, Ariel.

A kind of nest for security and for inspiration: call it squirrelling, or jackdaw-picking, but when I saw a photograph of a caddis fly in a book of my son's called *Animal Builders*, I recognized a kindred spirit. Here was this ungainly creature, covered in bric-à-brac, lumbering along with a jacket of scavengings patched all around its body. However, caddis fly hoarding isn't by any means sufficient to the task of making a story; the talismans and *aide-mémoires* have to connect to the central body, to its movement, its character, its meaning.

For *Indigo*, I proceeded in a similar fashion to my previous novel, *The Lost Father*, as well as, to some extent, my historical study of the Virgin Mary back in the seventies: I quarried my own family story, my antecedents, my social background, my education. My father's family were Creoles, in the sense in which Creole is sometimes used – as West Indians descended from the early European settlers. Creoles now can be white, brown, black; my sister and I were surprised when my father (not just white, but old school tie, cricket, club in St James's) returned from a trip to Trinidad in the mid-sixties with a snapshot of himself with Cousin Suzy (he had lost his heart to Cousin Suzy) and she was black. I began researching the history of the British Empire's development in the Caribbean; and a very absorbing, distressing story it is, full of pirates and buccaneers, cruelty and waste, and mostly all driven by the hunger for sugar. The trade in this commodity was so gigantic that the production, acquisition and consumption of sugar controlled national economies and the fate of people for three hundred years and still does, in a slightly less savage way today. (I put something sweet into almost every chapter of the book – stealthily – just to hint at how pervasively sugar flows through our world.)

I like research, I find the smell of book dust exciting, and libraries give me a sense of flight, so all my books are rooted in

reading. Many excellent studies of West Indian history helped me, as well as the astonishing accounts of early servants of Empire – soldiers, botanists and explorers, like the mercenary soldier W.J. Stedman's 'Narrative of an Expedition against the Revolted Negroes of Surinam', which Blake illustrated, to the brilliant anatomy of cricket and Empire, C.L.R. James's *Beyond a Boundary*. I enjoyed this part of the preparation for the book, for I was reading for the first time many living Caribbean writers as well. They gave me immeasurable inspiration as well as a new confidence in lyricism as a language of release, rebellion, self-affirmation. I have always felt abashed by my innate tendency to the lyric, and the rich, exuberant, visionary writings of poets like Aimé Césaire, Derek Walcott, Wilson Harris, Kenneth Kamau Brathwaite, Olive Senior – and in a more tense, bony mode, Jamaica Kincaid – freed me to trust in my native love of metaphor the long, singing line, the sensuous overkill rather than the English tradition of close-lipped irony and lean syntax. I sometimes think that my half-Italian blood (on my mother's side), plus the accident of my Francophone childhood (I went to French-speaking schools till I was ten), has made me a foreigner in England. Certainly when I first went to my convent boarding school in Berkshire I was ruthlessly teased for my odd mannerisms and my funny way of talking.

The literature of the Caribbean has grown up to one side of the metropolitan canon, as both Walcott and C.L.R. James have examined in their own work, but it has evolved a literature that is distinct and autonomous, which reflects the motley and the uprootedness of the different peoples there. As migration has become, it seems to me, the exemplary contemporary condition, with so many people on the move, voluntarily and involuntarily; and as the novel is above all a form in which crossing borders, entering new territories, trespassing and fence-mending can help make up new identities, the history of the Caribbean can teach us directly about the past and metaphorically about the future. I suppose that the hope for change is one of the dynamics of my writing, present

in both the history and the fiction. When Angela Carter wrote, in her introduction to *The Virago Book of Fairy Tales*, that such stories were composed in a spirit of 'heroic optimism', I recognized something in that phrase that I want from books: open-eyed truth-telling, but buoyed by belief that something just might give way to something better.

My Catholic girlhood taught me two disciplines that are invaluable, I think, for writing: the daily examination of conscience and the meditation on holy pictures. In some senses, I still practise these methods, profanely, to bring to life the caddis fly inside its higgledy-piggledy pile of scraps. In order to imagine the people in *Indigo* I sifted everything I could remember I had done or others had done, all our 'words and deeds'. I traced thoughts and actions over the days, over the years, in order to calibrate the characters' relations with one another, to weigh motive and justification, ends and means. At the same time, another, truly devotional practice has had an almost greater influence on me: prayers like The Stations of the Cross, which demand contemplating Christ's sufferings, or the Rosary, which conjures Mary's joys and sorrows and glories – with the help of images taken from a range of materials, from Raphael to the German sentimental ceramicist Hummel (who was a great favourite with the nuns) – trained me to imagine scenes and their accompanying grief and/or pleasure with intense, inner vividness. If the writing is going well, I can feel I'm racing to transcribe in words a picture scrolling in front of my eyes.

Italo Calvino, in his last series of lectures, *Six Memos for the Next Millennium*, describes how he used to pore over comic strips obsessively before he could read, and how his stories later grew out of images – the tarot pack in *The Castle of Crossed Destinies*, for instance. He was trying to create, he writes, '"a fantastic iconology" . . . I have adopted the method of telling my own stories, starting from pictures famous in the history of art or at any rate pictures that have made an impact on me.' When I read this I was delighted: I had always worried that my finding my

starting point in images, or mythological themes and figures was somehow incorrect for a contemporary writer, that proper fiction should begin with Real Life. In fact, I have been writing a series of short stories since the seventies inspired by paintings (the most recent being Tiepolo's *Moses in the Bulrushes*, which I combined with the reports of the sale of Romanian orphans). *Indigo*, too, has many familiar myths, taken from paintings, worked into the story: Titian's *Diana and Callisto* gave me the form for Sycorax's cruel rejection of Ariel when she becomes pregnant, for instance. I also realized, after I finished *Indigo*, that like all my novels, it shared a bipartite structure – that the past is recapitulated in the present, with variations that I hope are telling. This too, I have to admit, rises out of Catholic teaching: the New Covenant (the present day) fulfills the enigmatic prophecies of the Old (the past) in a typological pattern that seems to be etched into my mind. In *Indigo*, the Everard family attempt to repeat their colonial enterprise of the seventeenth century with tourist development today, and Sycorax, who embodies the island, even though her voice is imprisoned and muffled, survives in an altered form to bring about the defeat of these plans and an almost happy ending – at least one filled with hope and reconciliation, a kind of salvation.

Calvino, also in *Six Memos* (it's a wonderful handbook for writers) lists the qualities he desires and enjoys in literature: Lightness, Quickness, Exactitude, Visibility, Multiplicity, Consistency. I remember, during a retreat one term at the convent, that we were all told a story about Saint Thérèse of Lisieux, the Little Flower, who was shown on Christmas a trunkful of toys and asked to choose one for herself. She said, 'I want them all.' Oddly, in the crooked way of parables, the nun explained that this revealed Thérèse's great-heartedness, her appetite for the total experience which made her such a tremendous saint. Well, we were sceptical then and I still am. But the lesson went home.

I want them all, too: Lightness, Quickness, Exactitude and so on. But I would add, to the bundle of pickings in my caddis-fly cocoon: Sexuality, Richness, Humour, Anger, Doubt and Mercy.

GROWING A TALE
Hilary Mantel

I have sat, at the moment of purest heartbreak, in mental
agony, and put my thoughts on paper, and then I have taken
those thoughts and allocated them to one of my characters,
largely for comic effect.

Hilary Mantel's novels include *Every Day is Mother's Day*, *Vacant Possession* and *Eight Months on Ghazzah Street*. Her novel, *Fludd*, won the Winifred Holtby Memorial Prize, the Cheltenham Festival Literature Prize and the Southern Arts Literature Prize. Her most recent novel, *A Place of Greater Safety*, won the *Sunday Express* Award.

A couple of years ago I went to see a palmist. I could claim this was because I was preparing a short story about the prediction business – which is true – but to be completely honest I was hoping that she might see something nice in my palm, like dollar signs. 'This is a good solid practical hand,' she said. 'But oh dear . . . you haven't got much imagination, have you?'

Later, when she elicited the information that I was a novelist by profession, she was not abashed. 'I've read Barbara Cartland's palm,' she said. 'And it's nothing like yours.'

The funny thing is that I agree with her, and not just about my lack of resemblance to Babs. I don't think I have much imagination. What talent I have is for seeing the connections between things, and in finding a dramatic form for abstract ideas. It seems to me that my books are ideas-driven – they are a dramatic expression of what interests me or preoccupies me or obsesses me at the time. In other words, I don't cry 'I've thought of a great plot' or 'I've created a good character', I think 'This is interesting, how can I prevail upon the great world to listen to my little thoughts on it?'

I used to consider this lack of imagination a great drawback, because I wouldn't be able to think of plots that would hold the reader. I worried over 'plot' as if every book had to be a detective story, full of twists and turns and with no loose ends. I have heard other people who are beginning to write agonize over the same imaginary difficulty.

The comfort I offer is this: the elements of a book are not separable. When you eventually find the courage to begin work,

you will find that incident and character present themselves together. But if you aspire to a book that will last, that will be worth rereading, don't think about plot at all, think about your characters. (I must say at once that many of the characters in my own books are two-dimensional, vehicles for ideas or jokes. All that matters to me is that they do their jobs.) If you make your characters properly they will simply do what is within them, they'll act out the nature you have given them, and there – you'll find – you have your plot.

It is not so much plot as shape we have to find: something which offers dramatic satisfaction, which offers a slight improvement on what we perceive of the messiness of real life. Though actually, I don't believe real life is messy at all. If you keep a diary for a few years you'll see the order emerge. In a novel you simply proffer this order in a short form.

Don't misunderstand me: I have no time for people who talk in a vaguely mystical way about characters 'taking over'. If your characters have taken over there is something wrong with your book and something pretty seriously wrong with you. I think what these people are trying to say is that things have been written without much (apparent) premeditation, that the writer has performed certain work without being quite conscious of doing it. That is as it should be. It seems to me that a good part of the business of fiction is performed half-consciously, even subconsciously.

I have never based a character on a real person. Some are totally invented but most are composites, made up of a bit of this person and a bit of that. I'm sure this is true of most authors. I have not found that I select consciously the bits and pieces I'll use; a character simply arrives in my mind, and it may take me weeks or months to work out where the real-life origins lie. Almost always the origins lie in people who have passed through my life quickly, who have been on the periphery of it, whom I have hardly known at all. It is generally supposed that authors have a great interest in people, but I think I am unobservant about them,

almost incurious. I don't usually have an opinion about people, I find, unless they are strikingly congenial or strikingly unpleasant. But if I think a person is turning into a character, I will turn a different quality of attention on them.

I am also fond – like most writers, I suppose – of listening to the conversation of strangers. It is supposed that what you glean is of incidental benefit, and perhaps supplies a line or two. Not necessarily; it may lead to a whole book. In 1975 I was standing at a bus-stop reading a John Updike story, and along came two women continuing a conversation which was, as far as I could make out, about the goings-on at a local youth club. One of them said, 'They stole my skeleton, you know.'

The other said, 'Yes – good job it wasn't a full-sized one.'

Quite naturally, this preyed on my mind. It was rather like Beachcomber's SIXTY HORSES WEDGED IN A CHIMNEY: 'The story to this sensational headline has not turned up yet.' It took me ten years to do it, but I did eventually, in *Vacant Possession*, find a context in which a group of unruly children ranged about the north of England with a set of bones that weren't rightfully theirs and weren't full-sized.

When I am putting a book together my aim is never to think about plot, to think even less about structure. I like to let these things sort themselves out; to think a good deal about the people in my books, but much less about other issues. Line by line, writing's not so hard. You put in a comma, then you move it somewhere. You do a little sentence and then another little sentence. It's when you allow yourself to think of the totality of what you have to do, of the task which faces you with each book, that you feel it's hard, even terrifying. In my daily work, minimizing the terror is my object.

So how are characters built? How, come to that, does anything get done at all? It took me two books to find out how I work best, but now I have got a system that I shall probably stick with.

When you begin the work on a book – mentally, before anything goes down on paper – you have a lot of ideas, I find, that you

know are something to do with the book, but which don't seem to relate to each other. You may find a location that seems of interest – or a name may pop into your head – or a phrase. It is important to capture these insights. I carry small notebooks, which I can easily tear pages from: or I carry 3 x 5 inch index cards. I try to put down every insight, every glimpse of what this book will be, even if it's only a word.

When I have a few of these cards I pin them up on a cork notice-board in the room where I work. You do not know at this stage what is important – that will emerge. You do not know the order of events – but you don't need to know. Ideas build around these glimpses, these key phrases. Perhaps I write something else on one of my cards, just a few words; or perhaps the original idea begins to develop, and I am moved to write a paragraph or two. I pin that paragraph behind the card to which it relates.

The little words breed – sometimes several hundred offspring. I keep them on the board, in any order, until one day I see a sequence, a logic, begin to emerge. Then I repin them, very approximately, very roughly, in the order in which I think the narrative will shape. A few weeks on, all these bits of paper – the original cards, and anything that has accumulated behind them – go into a ring-binder. With a ring-binder you can easily swap the papers around – you're still not committing yourself to an order of events. You can add pages, transpose pages. But now you can begin to see how much of your book you have written. Some incidents, behind their original card, will be fully described, and some characters will come complete with their biographies, snatches of dialogue, their appearance and their way of talking. Other parts of the book will not have 'written themselves' at all – they await focused attention. But you know – indeed, you can see – how much work you have to do.

This method is soothing. Its virtue is that you never write yourself into a cul-de-sac; you have flexibility. Until you sit down to write your first draft sequentially, you have not committed yourself to linear narrative. I am amazed at how easily ideas fall

into place, how they multiply, if you give them a chance, and if you don't close off their possibilities too early. This is really a method of growing a book, rather than writing one.

I don't know whether this method might suit other people. It's the principle of it which is important, rather than whether you actually use index cards, notice boards, ring-binders. The principle is that you take the pressure off yourself. You stop worrying. Obviously in the course of putting together any novel you are going to encounter problems, and the temptation is to tackle them in the way that we are taught as children to tackle our problems: grit teeth, nose to grindstone, shoulder to wheel, bang head against brick wall, etc.

All this is a waste of effort. Determination is of great use to a novelist in search of a publisher, or to one who is pursuing research, or one who is pressured by a deadline, but it is irrelevant when what you have to solve is a creative problem. What you need then is an ability most of us acquire rather late in life – an ability to relax, let go. You trust and believe that there is an answer. You go for a walk, go to sleep. The answer is inside you somewhere, and will present itself. If it doesn't, after some days, you must consider whether you are asking the right question.

The planning stage of a book takes me a long time. I go through a phase where I know what is to happen, and to whom – and at this stage I can write a synopsis if it is needed – but I don't quite know what the book is *about*. I have not teased out all its themes. I tease them out through the act of writing itself. I am very seldom conscious of the metaphors I may embed in a book, of recurring images, of the links that (for a reader) hold a book together and give it integrity and a characteristic tone. To put it another way, half the time I don't know what I'm doing. The main thing I wonder about other writers – the thing I would really like to know – is how far they calculate and plan their effects, how deliberate is their method.

When I come to the stage of actual writing, the most important part of the working day is the ten minutes or so before I am fully

awake. In this state the day's work is planned and predicated, the mood and tone is set. However, if I have a particular problem, the solution often presents itself about an hour before dawn, I find; it wakes me up.

At this hour one writes easily, without strain or effort. There is no sense of the words being graven in stone, or of that sense of making a commitment that can be so paralysing. Sometimes what is written at this hour isn't used, but it is invariably free from constraint. It is at this time of day that someone who is beginning to write can learn to hear her own voice, find her tone. The defences are down; you are not self-conscious. You don't, in this bridge between waking and sleeping life, find there is a critic looking over your shoulder.

If I ever came to a time when I didn't know what to write, when I felt 'blocked', I would choose this time of day to find my voice again. How appallingly virtuous it sounds! I don't intend that it should. I'm not at all a person who is good at getting up in the morning or who has lots of energy. I'd sleep twelve hours a day if I weren't afraid of people's opinions.

There are other things I'd do, prescriptions I would hand myself for the writer's ideal life. In my ideal life I would spend an hour a day – split into two periods – in meditating, because I think that if I took meditation more seriously I would be twice as productive. I would spend another hour in the very different activity of thinking. Busyness, I feel increasingly, is the writer's curse and downfall. You read too much and write too readily, you become cut off from your inner life, from the flow of your own thoughts, and turned far too much towards the outside world. You take up busyness, I suppose, so that your daily work looks more like other people's. At various times you are ashamed of being a writer.

I said a book can be grown, rather than written, but if you do manage to persuade your mind to work for you in this way you have to accept the disadvantage, which is that you are never off duty; growing doesn't stop. The very least part of your writing is

what you do at your desk. Writers, so far as I can see, never have holidays. Once the process of becoming a writer is under way you can't stop it. Once you have begun, everything in the world is filtered through your writer's perception. You don't have a life any more; you just have writing opportunities. Things don't happen to you; you generate material. At the worst, you don't have friends, you have characters. This is why I say you can feel bad about writing. It is a cannibalistic process. That it can bring order, beauty and pity into the world I do not deny. But I myself am more conscious of my methods than my effects and I do not always admire my methods. I have sat, at the moment of purest heartbreak, in mental agony, and put my thoughts on paper, and then I have taken those thoughts and allocated them to one of my characters, largely for comic effect. On the whole I would guess that writers are ruthless people, though their saving grace is that they are ruthless with themselves.

I find it hard to generalize about my methods and motivations because my books are so different. Nothing I say about my methods applies to my earliest book, *A Place of Greater Safety*, which I first finished in 1979 and which I revised for publication during the summer of 1991.

I started this book in 1974, when I was twenty-two, though I started it in my head many years before that. It is a book about the French Revolution – I say about, rather than set in, because it lacks the conventional furniture of the historical novel. When I was twenty-two I didn't want to be a writer – I wanted to write this book. When the first version of it was finished I approached one publisher who didn't want to look at it and another who did but who then rejected it – quite properly, I think, because it is a very long book and would have been a huge commitment to make to an unknown author. (At this stage the only thing I had published was one short story, in *Punch*.)

The rejection of this book coincided with a personal crisis; I'd been ill for some years with an undiagnosed condition, and suddenly I got a diagnosis and found myself in hospital for

surgery. When I emerged my world had been overturned and I was not even sure I was the same person at all. I put my book aside and wrote another book; this was *Every Day is Mother's Day*, the first novel I published.

I mention this not to solicit sympathy, but because when I look at my motivation for writing – and even at my day-to-day routines – it is a major factor. I have never been able to recover health completely, and writing is a job that not-very-healthy people can do. You make your own routines and judge what to demand of yourself. If I had been fitter, perhaps I might have been a travel writer – but then again I might have had some other career entirely. A chance combination of circumstances has made me a novelist; writers are made, I think, not born.

A Place of Greater Safety was, of course, a research project as well as a writing project, and so evidence and material came in fragments, and had to be fitted together. Later, therefore, this seemed to me to be a natural way to write. It is not for me to say whether *A Place of Greater Safety* is a successful book or not, but writing it in its first version taught me a lot. The material I had was complicated and at times seemed intractable. Because I did manage to dramatize it for the reader, without taking easy ways out and distorting the known facts, I developed a confidence that in the making of a book every problem has a solution. It was also at this time that I set my own technical limits. I like to write in scenes, rather than in a smooth, easy flow of narrative. I also break all the rules about when one should use dialogue; I use it all the time, to push the story forward and define character.

I would say that my first book shows the cramping futility of that neat little adjuration to 'write what you know'. I'd rather say, write to find out – write to see what you know. You may surprise yourself.

This takes me back to my earlier point about qualities one needs and doesn't need. I get vaguely annoyed when people say 'you must be very self-disciplined to be a writer' – as if I were some sort of bond-servant, but indentured to myself. If you want

to do it, you do it; if you don't, you don't. Beyond that, it doesn't take any more self-discipline to a be writer than it does to get out of bed every morning when the alarum rings and go to an office or a factory year after year. Once it becomes the way you earn your living, the question of self-discipline is irrelevant.

In my view the most helpful personal quality a writer can cultivate is self-confidence – arrogance, if you can manage it. You write to impose yourself on the world, and you have to believe in your own ability when the world at large shows no sign of agreeing with you. A book isn't quickly achieved and the road to publication can be strewn with obstacles. It is especially important to be self-confident if you have no contacts and do not know other writers. If you are unpublished, you can still say to yourself, 'I am a writer.' You should define yourself as such. Of course, people will laugh at you, but he who laughs last, etc. Many people – women especially – feel guilty about writing. They feel it is self-indulgent. But it is not. It is a way of coming to grips with the world, and it is also a way of making money.

That sums up, really, the two things I think about writing – one is that it is a strange, remote, singular and mysterious business, and the other is that it *is* a business and it pays the bills. My bank statements are very important to me, but so are my dreams. In *Vacant Possession* I included two characters – Sholto Marks and Emmanuel Crisp – who had appeared to me in a dream some years before. In my novel, they were patients from a mental hospital, released to wreak well-deserved havoc in 'the community'; in my dream they were two men in an underground bunker, singing selections from something called *The Disaster Songbook*. I hadn't thought of making them into characters, but soon after I began *Vacant Possession* I saw Emmanuel Crisp – *in propria persona* in flesh-and-blood form – travelling second class on the train between Windsor and London Waterloo. He was complete in every detail: his remote other-worldly expression, the woolly snake of hair that wound about his pate. I thought it was a signal that I should put him in my book.

When you start explaining things like this to people – that, like it or not, this is how it is done – they think you're mad. Perhaps you are. But as you sit down each day to work you have to conceal this fact from yourself. The time for paranormal phenomena and cork notice-boards has passed. You now proceed with a cool, calculating sobriety, as if you were making up your quarterly accounts. You just put a comma. Then perhaps you move it. Just one little word. Then just another.

IMAGINATION AND EXPERIENCE
Brian Moore

Fiction is not the story of my life or the lives of people I have known. It is a struggle to write novels which will in some way reflect my own experience through the adventures of my characters, novels which permit me to re-examine beliefs I no longer hold and search for some meaning in my life.

Brian Moore is the Belfast-born author of sixteen novels. His 1987 novel, *The Colour of Blood*, was short-listed for the Booker Prize. His most recent novel is *No Other Life*.

IMAGINATION AND EXPERIENCE

This is from Henri Troyat's biography of Leo Tolstoy. It deals with the period of Tolstoy's life when he had begun to write *Anna Karenina*.

... he laboured away at his manuscript, full of mistrust, anger and weariness. He made revision after revision. He felt that he was taking two steps backward for one step ahead. 'There are days when one gets up feeling refreshed and clear-headed,' he said. 'One begins to write; everything is fine, it all comes naturally. The next day one reads it over, it all has to go because the heart isn't there. No imagination, no talent. That *quelque chose* is lacking without which our intelligence is worthless. Other days one gets up, hating the world, nerves completely on edge; nevertheless, one hopes to be able to get something done. And indeed, it doesn't go too badly; it's vivid, there is imagination by the carload. Again, one reads it over: meaningless, stupid; the brains weren't there. Imagination and intelligence have to work together. As soon as one or the other gets the upper hand, all is lost. There is nothing to do but throw away what you've done and start over.'

Anyone who is a novelist knows that paragraph accurately describes the period in writing a novel when the characters and scenes refuse to move forward and the writer is in danger of suffering that accidie in which novels die. The elements which Tolstoy is trying to put in balance are what he calls imagination and intelligence. Imagination, we understand, but what is this 'intelligence' he speaks of? Is it the intelligence of a novelist who has written other novels and knows he has fallen off the tightrope which he must walk in order to keep the story alive and suspend

the reader's disbelief? I think it is. But it is also something else. It is the faculty of balancing the fiction one is writing against the facts of one's life and the lives of people one knows.

And so we come back to the question of experience – the hand which real life has dealt us and which some of us attempt to play out in our novels. Unfortunately, for most of us, there are not enough cards in this hand to sustain a career. Most of us, unlike Tolstoy, do not lead interesting lives and if, like me, you have been a novelist, and nothing but a novelist for many years you have long ago ceased to live anything like a normal existence. You have no regular job, you spend most of your days alone in a room, you do not have a communal workplace which allows you to observe the behaviour of other people. If you have friends they tend to be other writers, academics, actors – people who, as Flaubert pointed out, are not 'dans le vrai' – living lives which correspond to the lives of the majority of your readers. So you are at double risk. Your characters, creatures invented by you, assume an ever-increasing importance in your life. If you continue to write novels and do little else, some sort of élan vital drains out of you. If what Tolstoy called 'intelligence' means experience of real life, you are no longer a front-line witness.

I think this feeling of isolation, this distancing of oneself from real life, is the reason so many people write one or two novels and then stop and become teachers, dramatists, scriptwriters or pundits. And the problem is exacerbated by the fact that we no longer live in a cohesive society as did the great nineteenth-century novelists. We cannot assume that our readers will follow us confidently into the worlds we write about as did the readers of Balzac and Dickens. It becomes more and more difficult to create a realistic novelistic universe.

But let's go back to Tolstoy for a moment.

Tolstoy, unlike most novelists, lived a full life. He was an aristocrat, who had fought bravely in distant military campaigns. In his youth he was a gambler, reckless to the point of almost losing his inheritance, a womanizer, a heavy drinker, irresponsible,

self-centred, often dissolute. But he also had the soul of a saint, a flawed saint who railed against injustice and yearned for a purer existence, but who did not free his own serfs and lived comfortably on the profits of his estates. Despite this, his teachings affected hundreds of thousands of people and at the time of his death he was an international figure, and probably the most influential novelist who ever lived.

Yet in the most interesting period of his life – the fifteen years in which he did his greatest work as a novelist – he did NOT use his former life directly in his novels. In fact, that novel – *Anna Karenina* – which was giving him so much difficulty, was set in motion by his chancing to hear of a woman, the mistress of a neighbour, who had thrown herself under a train because her lover had been neglecting her and planned to marry his children's German governess. Troyat tells that the day before this woman killed herself she sent a note to her lover. 'You are my murderer. Be happy, if an assassin can be happy. If you like, you can see my corpse on the rails at Yasenki.' That was on 4 January 1872. The following day Tolstoy went to the station as a spectator while the autopsy was being performed in the presence of a police inspector. Staring at the ugly mutilated body, he tried to imagine the existence of this woman who had died a senseless death for the sake of love.

Imagination. A chance remark, a newspaper clipping, an over-heard story. How often are these slight-seeming things the genesis of a novel. But almost always it seems that this synthesis occurs because these things connect with the novelist's preoccupations – I might say obsessions. Infidelity and violent death. These were subjects which had been in Tolstoy's mind for some time. A few years earlier he told his wife Sonya that he wanted to write about an upper-class woman guilty of adultery. Sonya wrote in *her* diary: 'He told me that the whole problem, for him, was to make the woman pitiable but not contemptible and that when this creature came into his mind as a type, all the masculine characters he had previously invented grouped themselves around her.'

And then, that morning in the railway station, looking at the dead body of a woman who was not upper class, a discarded mistress, not guilty of adultery, but who had died an ugly foolish death to revenge herself on the lover who had forsaken her, the magical moment occurred. Imagination and intelligence suddenly came together. The hard work lay ahead, the frustrations, the delays, the weariness, the despair which he experienced in the writing of *Anna Karenina*. But the obsession had taken hold of him and would not leave him. Imagination and intelligence did not desert him. The result was a masterpiece.

And it is imagination, the ability to become characters very different from oneself, which differentiates him from lesser writers. He started by writing about 'a woman who was pitiable but not contemptible', but as he continued to write and as he made the imaginative leap into the character's mind, he actually fell in love with Anna. It is this quality of empathy which makes it one of the great novels. And this is what I find fascinating. Fifteen years later the novel was long dead in his mind. When praised for this work he seemed to regret having written it and dismissed it as a tawdry tale of adultery. He had forgotten his love affair with Anna.

And in that final rejection and misunderstanding of his work Tolstoy proved to be a true novelist. For when a novel is finished and the printed book arrives with a joyful note from the publisher, the true novelist begins to forget what he has written. When the act of writing is over, imagination and intelligence desert him and his opinions on the merits of his book have no more weight than the opinions of anyone else.

Having said that, I should stop writing, for if you believe that statement, and I do, there is nothing intelligent I can say about my own work. But perhaps I can discuss briefly something which I have experienced: the life of a novelist self-exiled from his own country who discovered, after he had written three novels set in his birthplace, that he could no longer dwell comfortably in that past. When I wrote my first novel I was 26 years old and had emigrated to Canada. I had spent some years in Italy, France and

Poland and yet it did not occur to me to write about those places. My literary hero at the time was Joyce who had managed to write his entire *œuvre* about Dublin, a city which he had abandoned in his twenties to live permanently in Europe. When I started to write I too wrote about the place of my birth. But my birthplace was Belfast. And, unlike Joyce, I remembered my native city with a mixture of anger and bitterness which made me want to write it out of my system and look for a new world in which I and my characters could live. From then on, from time to time Ireland would appear in my novels, but it was not until 1989 that I returned to Belfast as the setting for one of my books. In my third novel, *The Luck of Ginger Coffey*, my character and I emigrated to Canada and later my novels followed the course of my emigration, moving on with me to New York and California. But by the time I had written my fourth novel – which was set in New York – I knew that my books could no longer follow the mundane events of my existence. From that time on, each novel was, for me, a new beginning. I was forced to rely on imagination and experimentation.

Luckily, I had begun to read Borges, a writer whose work was totally different from my own. I saw how he created imaginary worlds which seemed totally real. How the fantastic could be made to seem mundane, simply through the skill of his writing. And so in some way I broke free from the realism of my early novels. Since then each work has been, for me, a new beginning. I have written an adventure tale in the Conradian manner, metaphysical thrillers, allegorical fantasies, and novels in which the natural and the supernatural co-exist in dangerous proximity. What I am trying to say is that my life in exile has forced me to become a literary chameleon. I sometimes wonder what would have happened to me had I not left Ireland, had I continued to write novels based on the world I was born into, as have many of my contemporaries. I will never know what I may have lost by self-exile. I suspect that I might by now be in the state which is described by Paul Valéry: 'The writer consumes everything he is

and everything around him. His pleasures and griefs, his business, God, his childhood, his wife, his friends and enemies, his knowledge and ignorance, all are tossed onto the fateful paper.' But this is the same Valéry who said: 'I cannot write a novel because I could never write the sentence, "The Marquise left the house at five o'clock."' Exactly. That sort of sentence is, for me, at the heart of novel writing and if it offends you, forget about writing novels. The novel tells a story. The story is located in time and place. The story is fiction. It can never be true, but to succeed as art it must inspire belief.

And so, for me, fiction is not the story of my life or the lives of people I have known. It is a struggle to write novels which will in some way reflect my own experience through the adventures of my characters, novels which permit me to re-examine beliefs I no longer hold and search for some meaning in my life. The writing of novels has become my *raison d'être* – a surrogate existence, if you will. And in the years I have been writing novels I have remained deaf to the literary wars which have been going on over my head – the New Critics, the anti-*roman*, the *nouveau roman*, Derrida, Lacan, deconstruction. They do not seem to deal with these questions of imagination and intelligence which I believe to be at the heart of all fiction.

The German poet Novalis wrote that 'the greatest sorcerer would be the one who cast a spell on himself to the extent of taking the creations of his imagination for autonomous apparitions, as we do in our dreams'. He also wrote that 'genius is the capacity to deal with imagined objects as with real ones and to accord them the same kind of treatment. It differs from the talent to present something, to observe it exactly and to give a fitting account of the things observed.'

We are not geniuses, most of us who write novels, but we are, many of us, people who have chosen to live the surrogate life of the imagination. We have, perhaps, settled for that state which Wallace Stevens speaks of. 'The final belief,' he said, 'is to believe in a fiction which you know to be a fiction, there being nothing else.'

GRACEFUL COMBINATIONS

Malcolm Bradbury

In Britain, creative writing has often had a suspect reputation among academics, and is sometimes thought of as rather like playing in the sand in primary school, perhaps good in encouraging self-expression, but adding little in the way of knowledge or experience.

Malcolm Bradbury is a Professor of American Studies at the University of East Anglia and teaches an M.A. course in creative writing there. He is the author of several acclaimed novels, including *Rates of Exchange*, which was short-listed for the Booker Prize, and *The History Man*, which won the Royal Society of Literature Award. His most recent novel is *Doctor Criminale*.

GRACEFUL COMBINATIONS

Like many people these days I am a person with two professions. For one part of the year I am a full-time writer, working as a novelist, critic and television playwright, and earning my way in the writer's market-place. For another part I am a university professor, teaching the novel and theory, Dickens and Derrida, and making my way in the campus market-place, as it has increasingly come to be. Part of the year I perform the quiet and lonely task of writing, sitting down every morning in front of the typewriter or now word processor, surrounded by coffee cups and creative tension, drawing on the strange inner funds that compel writers, throughout history, to write. And part of the year I become the critical reader and theorist, sitting down in some seminar room, surrounded by dead cardboard teacups and No Smoking signs, dissecting such serious theoretical questions as whether there is, conceptually speaking, any such thing as an author, a text, a discourse, a reader.

This particular combination of activities became my life at the very end of the fifties, when I published my first novel and also took my first academic job. It was a familiar enough situation in the post-war years, at a time when the pre-war era of modernist experiment and foreign bohemias had slipped away, and the new centre of writing was becoming, increasingly, the university campus. This was very clearly true in the United States, where I spent several of my postgraduate years. It was a time of university expansion and of literary contraction, when a writer's living was becoming ever harder to come by. It was also a time when university literature departments were departing from historical

language study and showing an increasing willingness to include contemporary literature in their programmes, and when there were new bridges being built between contemporary writing and criticism. Indeed, criticism and creation seemed happy companions for each other. Many of the leading American critics were themselves writers: John Crowe Ransom, Robert Penn Warren, Allen Tate, Howard Nemerov, and many more. In Britain too there were similar graceful combinations: Kingsley Amis, John Wain, Iris Murdoch, Anthony Burgess, Donald Davie, and many more were both writers and university teachers.

This hardly seemed a novelty. Many of the most notable and interesting authors of the earlier part of the twentieth century had been both writers and critics of very high distinction. Ezra Pound and T.S. Eliot, W.H. Auden and Stephen Spender, William Empson and I.A. Richards preached what they practised and practised what they preached. The post-war incorporation of the writer on to the campus was the extension and, of course, to some degree the institutionalization of a process that had been evolving throughout the century, the systematization of the arts within the professions. If the financial virtues of the situation were obvious (what poet makes a living in Britain?), the intellectual ones seemed even more substantial. It seemed obvious that the study of literature was enlarged by contact with and the reflections and analyses of those who were practitioners. In fact, it seemed in many ways hard to imagine a practice of criticism which was not interlinked with and illuminated by the practice of writing itself.

From my own point of view the intimacy was ideal. A writer is, after all, a reader, probably an indefatigable one. The acquisition of a tradition, the attention to the contemporary, the preoccupation with literary and aesthetic theory, the concern with the nature of discourse and the structure of narrative that is essential to the writer is equally essential to the critic, and vice, of course, versa. From the point of view of literature (or English) as a subject, the rewards seem equally apparent. The practice of writing ought ideally to develop (and it frequently does) those inward

awarenesses, those literary insights, those conceptions of imaginative discovery, that should pass onward into all critical reflection. The two worlds of my life ought to balance each other with perfect elegance, as reader balances writer, as decoder balances coder. So, for much of the time, they do. The dual role pleases me, and I would not freely give up either part of it. It is often argued (again on a television programme lately) that the ideal 'other' job for a writer (and most writers indeed need other jobs) is one not connected with writing or literature but with life itself: gardening, working in a mental hospital. But for myself the passage from writing to reading, teaching and literary study seems endlessly enlarging, and the one activity indeed grows into and out of the other.

This much said, I then have to admit that in many matters at least the relation between the writer and the academic critic and theorist of literature seems to me to have grown ever more strained over my writing and teaching lifetime, during which the conditions both of writing and of academic life have changed greatly. There are several very obvious reasons for this. On the side of writing, first: the era of the financially and aesthetically independent writer has largely passed, and writing has increasingly become an aspect of commerce. In this it has grown increasingly accountable to an ever more corporate and planned market-place, a broad media process in which self-presentation is often more important than a climate of criticism. Writers generally lack an experimental or inquiring setting in which to devote themselves, as Pound or Eliot did, to criticism or theory. They are small businesses, part of the late bourgeois army of the self-employed, and frequently have a cautiously private attitude towards their own artistic properties and property. The independent artistic debate which once surrounded the more serious part of writing has itself plainly diminished. So, in an age uncomfortable with élitist concepts, has all talk of 'standards'. In public debate, criticism has grown vastly more partial and arbitrary. At the same time as writers have grown more commercial, publishing expectations have often become far more generic and conventional.

The change in what used to be called criticism and is now called literary theory is even greater. Here I mean what is taught academically as criticism, particularly in the universities. The growth of English or literature as a university subject (in Britain, at least, it remains one of the most applied for of academic subjects) has been vast, and it has deeply changed in character. It is, after all, the life work of a large salaried academic bureaucracy, with its own career goals and prospects. It is ambitious both to justify and give the substance of theory to its discipline. The passage from what is now rejected as the 'New Criticism' to the new era of Literary Theory is an essential part of this process. The 'New Criticism', which in practice would include the work of many of those writer–critics whom I mentioned earlier, along with figures like W.K. Wimsatt, Cleanth Brooks, I.A. Richards and F.R. Levis, was not itself short of theory. In fact, if we take a simple progressive view of these things we could say that it was partly out of just this theory that much of the ever Newer Criticism has been born.

Why, asks Ralph Cohen, editing a recent anthology of international essays called *The Future of Literary Theory* (1989), do we need this volume? He answers: 'Because we are in the midst of rapid changes in the practice of literary theory and we need to understand why received views of formalism, of literary history, of literary language, of readers, writers and canons have come to be questioned, revised, or replaced.' These changes have been occasioned by 'the discoveries of deconstruction, psychoanalysis, feminism and history, of continental thinkers and scholars from other disciplines'. All this, we discover, constructs a 'new agenda', some of it very explicitly ideological in character. The construction of this agenda clearly precedes the reading of literature. The general presumption is that literature is a second-order activity forced to yield to a first-order activity, the elucidation and practice of literary theory itself. As one deconstructive (and sensitive) literary critic, Jonathan Culler, has proudly proclaimed, 'the history of literature now becomes part of the history of criticism.'

The new literary theory nowadays owes very little to the speculations and discoveries of literary practitioners, to the Coleridges and Eliots, the Shelleys and the Pounds. It owes most to certain lines of development in French and German philosophy, particularly to that strand of it now called Deconstruction. Since this foregrounds language as the centre of philosophical anxiety, but also meshes with certain large-scale historical proposals about the modern crisis of the subject, it reads, or rather interrogates or deconstructs, texts in a certain way. It validates creative misreading, and largely refuses to attend to the existential or humanistic content of literature. It frequently proposes the end of moral unity and the collapse of western humanism, and so reads contemporary literature in the light of an inclusive description about the historical state of affairs or, as it is increasingly expressed, the Postmodern Condition. Much of this is interesting, some of it influential with some of our better writers, like Italo Calvino or Umberto Eco. But it has only a little to do with the direct practice of writing, its stimulation, or indeed its profitable criticism.

I may possibly be under a lunatic delusion, but I believe I sense some change in this climate. Part of the problem of literary theory is that it has become implicated in the crisis of late twentieth-century European philosophy, or rather the crisis of a part of it. As one French philosopher, Philippe Lacoue-Labarthe, lately put it, 'the word philosophy now only designates the commentary on philosophy, or, where it claims to free itself from this, merely a more or less brilliant and coherent form of epigonal variation'. As philosophy now shows signs of striving to recover itself as philosophy, so literary theory or criticism may well begin striving to recover its intimacy with the creative, with the experiential nature of writing and its exploration of things imagined, or fictive. And I do see some signs – the growing academic interest in creative writing is one of them – that this is happening.

Over recent years what one influential deconstructive critic, Paul de Man, criticized as a 'resistance to theory' has seemed to some degree necessary as a way of insisting on literature, imaginative

writing, as a major mode of human investigation and discovery. De Man, who had a gift for irony, himself acknowledged that from time to time the resistance was highly desirable. Writers normally do well not to become enmeshed in totalistic explanations of language, text, and history, the business of critical commissariats; these rarely link in with the intimate experiences of writing. For the moment what criticism plainly lacks is a substantive theory of creativity itself – a concept of the ways in which the instincts, the structures, the modal forms of imaginative expression can take on their purpose and pattern not as textual slippage but as original humane discovery.

The ill-balanced relationship between contemporary writing and contemporary criticism has been, for me, one among many reasons for believing that creative writing has a significant place in the modern department of English or literature. Writers, as I have said, have for some time had a place on the university campus and in literature departments, though the numbers have generally diminished, in Britain at least. In the United States they have increasingly been there as teachers of creative writing. This is not always the best solution; it sometimes academicizes writing while at the same time separating the writer from the larger activities of the literature department. Nonetheless, many of the effects have been good, and much of the best and most serious writing in the United States has been supported on the campuses. In Britain, creative writing has often had a suspect reputation among academics, and is sometimes thought of as rather like playing in the sand in primary school, perhaps good in encouraging self-expression, but adding little in the way of knowledge, experience or, of course, theory.

I have a different view, after twenty years of interest in the subject. I think those universities that have also taken an interest have added to the stock of serious contemporary writing in Britain. Moreover, the benefits are mutual. In a time when the literary scene lacks environments and occasions for the thoughtful discussion and analysis of writing, the university has the power

and means to provide such a setting. The good writer is the good reader, and indeed needs some contact with the literary tradition and the current debates of criticism. And in a period when criticism has often placed itself apart from writers and their creative practice, the work under way in serious writing programmes – and in some cases it has been work of considerable importance – is a manifest example of the deep endeavour behind the writing process, a plain reminder that a work is the product of a living human agent, and not simply a text or a sign. For myself, the teaching of writers as well as readers has done a good deal to heal the sense of schizophrenia that can nowadays be part of the passage from the role of writer to the role of critic. In the end, every writer is a reader, and every reader is a critic. It is the task of all those who practise or study literature to have some strong sense of what all these functions are, and what they can become.

LITERATURE AND THE KITCHEN TABLE
Marilyn French

The young are still taught, as I was taught decades ago, that difficulty and opacity are marks of profundity ... I no longer believe any of this. Good writers produce 'inaccessible' work when they cannot be heard otherwise.

LITERATURE AND THE KITCHEN TABLE

Marilyn French

Marilyn French is the author of three acclaimed feminist novels, *The Bleeding Heart*, *The Women's Room* and *Her Mother's Daughter*. Her latest work, *The War Against Women*, a study of the worldwide oppression of women, is part of a forthcoming international history of women, *From Eve to Dawn*.

LITERATURE AND THE KITCHEN TABLE

I wrote all through my childhood, but not with the hope of publishing until 1956. At that time, I had a college degree, a husband, two babies, a tiny house in the suburbs, little experience of the world, and a vague unhappiness. I wrote poetic stories with an undertone of violent emotion. I knew that one reason for my misery was the sexual division of the world and its gender definitions: I was always a feminist. I had many arguments and won all my verbal battles, mainly because my opponents backed off, appalled or indifferent. But I daily lost the war to define myself and my own life.

I don't know if you understand the pain one suffers from something so abstract, so seemingly impersonal as social definition. I know from reading work by women of colour that they feel it intensely still. In my youth, all women were harmed by their social definition. Most were unhappy but few attributed their misery to that, holding their husbands, mothers-in-law, or tiny budgets responsible. It may sound self-exalting to say that the lack I felt most keenly was of a philosophy – an explanation of how the world had come to be arranged as it was (for it seemed insane to me) and a coherent critique of the dominant morality and social structure. But that is the case – without a philosophy, I couldn't think past certain boundaries, couldn't act positively. Without an ideological structure, rebellion is haphazard, personal, and largely negative in impact.

Since no such philosophy existed at the time, I tried to suggest the profound unhappiness of women obliquely. I sent out short stories and found an agent, who for a time thought my first novel

good enough to handle. Over the years I collected a most disparate set of rejection slips. All said I wrote well BUT: the buts were so varied that I couldn't learn anything from them.

I had had a male education – I was intellectually encouraged both at school and home, which is unusual for girls, and I read men almost exclusively, starting with Tom Paine, Schopenhauer, and Nietzsche at fourteen. I read women's work at school only in the lower grades – sweet little poems, most by Christina Rossetti. My college courses did not include a single woman novelist, poet, philosopher, playwright, historian, psychologist, anthropologist (not even Margaret Mead), or sociologist. I read Austen, Eliot, Woolf, Mansfield, Dickinson and (unfortunately) popular writers like Clare Booth Luce, but on my own. I understood that women writers were not as good as men.

I was intellectually lonely. I made up projects for myself, as 'make-work'. I read Greek philosophy, world history, and studied Renaissance art, but nothing yielded what I needed. I called a novel in progress *The Search for the Usable Past* until Henry Steele Commager (I think) used that title for a work of history. Over the years, my children grew, I went back to school for a master's degree and began to teach. Earning my own salary made it possible for me to divorce a husband who did not want a divorce, and in time, I left the suburbs for Cambridge, Massachusetts and Harvard, to study for a Ph.D. I published a few short pieces and in 1976, twenty years after I began writing seriously, published my first book – a critical study of James Joyce's *Ulysses* based on my dissertation.

By this time, an active women's movement was creating an intellectual base for both political and historical thought – a philosophy! I came to see that my education had made me an élitist, a person who believed that some people were *naturally* superior to others by virtue of their superior minds. To believe this, one must also believe that mind and body are separate and that body and emotion are base. One didn't have to read theory to learn this: ordinary people also found emotion degrading,

weakness contemptible, and body disgusting. *This*, I realized, was why I had felt such anguish at giving birth in 1953: giving birth is the ultimate bodily act. I recognized too that these beliefs did not reflect my own sense of things, that I had surrendered my personal take on experience to a set of received ideas.

Feminism ushered in the most fertile period of my life – one which has continued to the present. Feminism not only gave me a language for and an approach to my own experience but it liberated and empowered my mind by freeing it from the mystifications of patriarchal thought. In 1972, I started a novel about this mental liberation – about living without it and living with it, detailing what such a liberation *can* deliver and what it cannot.

I had long since concluded that male writers were deemed superior because their books were difficult to read. No woman wrote like Joyce, Pound, Faulkner, Malcolm Lowry, Julio Cortazar, or Jean Genet (all highly regarded in the 1960s): what woman could get away with writing like that? What critic would be willing to spend his life explicating a woman's novel? This idea that opacity was prestigious had affected the style of my early novels – I had allowed my confusions about the novel and the world's arrangements to stand, feeling they added ambiguity to my work.

But by the 1970s, I realized that opacity was not a value. It may have been necessary for Joyce or Pound, but now that feminism had illuminated the way of the world, it was not necessary for me. Moreover, the book I had in mind could not be written obliquely: it had to be explicit. I knew that explicitness would assault the dominant consciousness, whose representatives would attack without mercy, and would accuse me of writing a didactic novel. So be it, I decided.

I began what became *The Women's Room* in the summer of 1972, in Aspen. Trying to write a novel about the education of a person into full consciousness, that would draw in non-feminist readers, I used a male narrator, a young journalist who goes to Ohio to investigate the killing of a woman by police in a protest based on the Kent State massacre. I wrote over 150 pages, but it

never worked: the boy was too callow. I started again, with an ordinary housewife as narrator, a friend of the rebellious woman. But she was too blind. I put it aside again. I had a life – my children were away at college, I was teaching at a small liberal arts college, I had work, friends, lovers. But the novel stayed on my mind until one night the solution presented itself: I sat up straight in bed. I would split the narration between the narrator's enlightened and unenlightened consciousness. The next day I began the third draft and never faltered after that.

I used a completely new style: I wanted a tone, the voice of a woman sitting across a kitchen table from the reader, talking, not above the events, but immersed in them, unable easily to judge them because she was living them. Any authority she possessed was merely the authority of her own experience. She was equal, not superior to the reader, her language the ordinary language of the kitchen table, which does not lack its own elegance. And her experience, like most women's, required acknowledgement of the essential nature of 'women's work' and its virtual slavery – the sense of being utterly vital to society yet being treated by it as utterly inconsequential; the profundity of motherhood and its powerlessness; the importance of women's relations with each other in sustaining their despised but essential project and the common failure of those relations in a woman-despising world.

I knew that 'women's' work was illegitimate as a subject in literature: yet it is what 95% of the women in the world actually do a large part of the time. Literature had never treated seriously the most universal and necessary work on earth – to children, to men, to women: having and raising children, maintaining the home, doing the cooking and the laundry, cleaning, ministering to broken hearts and scraped knees. What I wanted the reader to undergo was the experience of being a person of no consequence treated by husband as servant and possession, unable to get a job that would support her and her children, brushed off by police, judges, doctors, psychiatrists – who suddenly starts to take *herself* seriously, to see herself as a human being who matters.

I also wrote a running commentary on traditional literature about women and men, on the falseness of happy endings for females, tragic ones for males, of ideals like chastity and fidelity and happiness within marriage (placed only on females), and of males as beings in control of themselves and others. One reason (I think) some reviewers found the male figures in *The Women's Room* wanting is because I showed men as only human beings with little control, who cannot 'save' women – or even themselves. *No one* can be saved because no one transcends the human condition: although traditional literature insists otherwise.

The Bleeding Heart asks the question whether decent relations are possible between women and men. As its title indicates, it is a commentary on romantic literature, so is written in the third person and has a seemingly traditional heroine and hero filling the traditional roles of sufferer and controller (victor). When I began, I had no clear ending, no final 'answer'. The ending grew out of the situation. *Her Mother's Daughter* examines in depth the relation between mothers and daughters, challenging both the sentimentalization of motherhood and the mother-hatred that infects our century. It has a dominant consciousness, but one without boundaries. Like actual mothers and daughters, its characters bleed into each other, becoming voices in a chorus.

In all my work I emphasize the centrality to human life and society of women's work of birth and child-rearing and maintenance and re-creation, unrewarded, even unsupported as they are. I insist that humans cannot transcend nature, can only delude themselves that transcendence is possible: total control even of self is not a human possibility and men have no more of it than women *by nature* – however much control laws and attitudes may give them. I try not to speak authoritatively but with a merely human voice to merely human readers, to urge them to consider their experience meaningful and empowering. The weight of the past is still heavy: the world still believes in hierarchy and worldly power, in the trappings that symbolize transcendence. It still follows its path to suicide. Literature that does not in some way

challenge these pernicious beliefs in some way colludes with them. I suspect we all collude with them willy-nilly.

The young are still taught, as I was taught decades ago, that difficulty and opacity are marks of profundity, that art is 'above' politics and exists for its own sake. I no longer believe any of this. Good writers produce 'inaccessible' work when they cannot be heard otherwise. No human act is 'above' any other; art is not useless, a parasitic élite feeding on the despised peasants and workers of society. Art is food for the heart, emotions, and mind, which are integrated and part of the body, and never lacks a political dimension. 'The poet' is not a superior being, but simply someone making something useful and beautiful – as all human productions could be, should be.

THE LANGUAGE OF CATS

Shena Mackay

There are days when it is impossible to look at, say, a tree against the sky, without the brain insisting on translating every nuance into words, and recently, unwell and with a high temperature, I was tortured by this question: how do cats think without language?

Shena Mackay is the Edinburgh-born author of seven novels and two volumes of short stories. Her works include *Redhill Rococo*, which won the 1987 Fawcett Prize, *Babies in Rhinestones* and *Dreams of Dead Women's Handbags*. Her most recent novel is *Dunedin*.

THE LANGUAGE OF CATS

The analogy between childbirth and producing a book does not really fit. The time-scale is wrong and the image of an author, especially a male author, brought to bed of a bouncing hardback is not a pretty one. Nevertheless, just like the woman who groans 'Never again!', the writer will forget the pain of delivery; it's Nature's Way. One advantage that the writer does have over the mother is the option of a sort of extended multiple birth; short stories which may be collected into a volume and which might, with luck and the right contract, earn their keep by appearing first in one of the too few magazines that publish fiction, or on the radio. That may sound mercenary but many writers live like Billy Bunter in expectation of a postal order which never comes (a rainforest of bills, junk mail and letters – some wonderful and a pleasure to answer, some not but requiring answers, manages to get through – and requests from good causes always arrive when you're penniless), and publishers usually prefer novels anyway.

Writing about writing, the act and thought processes of it, is difficult, and although Magritte's word-pictures are brilliant explorations of the relationship between images and written names, perhaps Gertrude Stein's brave but over-extended and ultimately unreadable attempt to do with words what the Cubists were doing with paint only demonstrates the problems. As the brain makes cross-references, cross-pollination occurs between words and horticultural metaphors mess up the electricals so that the writer has to seek distraction or take refuge in chores or checking yet again that there has been no unscheduled postal delivery. Writing about the mechanics is easier: that terrifying blank white

sheet of paper, the *tabula rasa* dusted with Floris talc, the Mont Blanc or Waterman pen, the specially ruled exercise books, the cork-lined shed or bedroom. Most of my own works have been composed in my round tower room, with a view of the white garden where Hadjie might be toying with a trug, while Violet vaults a distant stile, but relating working methods and circumstances cannot explain the impulse to write, why one still life or bit of dialogue and not another should act on the nervous system or come into the mind as if from nowhere, or why an idea which is so abstract at first that it is no more than a feeling, a blur of rainbow rollers in a carwash or windblown silver undersides of leaves, should declare itself as either an embryo novel or a short story. I have never started on a short story and found that it wanted to become a novel although I have often wished, when faced with the long labour of a novel, for the comparative ease of the short story.

I can describe the difference between starting a novel or a story only in visual terms (although very often I have the title and first and last sentences before the bits in the middle); climbing Everest as opposed to Ben Nevis, distances in a landscape, guessing rather than weighing the ingredients of a cake. Language – shapes coming out of people's mouths, symbols on paper, papyrus or stone (babies acquiring the astonishing accomplishment of speech) – is so mysterious, a magical toy for the writer to play with: for example, I might type the word *mandarin*, in relation to style, and see a tin of orange segments in heavy syrup or a nodding statuette or an oriental duck; I might look up *mandarin* in the dictionary and my eye might light on *mandolin* or *mandragora*; I might check the plumage (that phrase suggesting a gingham or tartan bird) of the mandarin duck and find myself reading about muscovies or Scottish soldier-like khaki Campbells. Or I could write *brain* and glance up at a jug of delicately lobed hydrangeas. When there is time and space for such essential mental pottering, for browsing in dictionaries, works of reference of all kinds, film and poetry books, being a writer is such fun. As Louis MacNeice said,

'World is crazier and more of it than we think,/Incorrigibly plural . . .' (that quotation gave a long and pleasurable excuse for getting lost in the *Collected Poems*, and I remember the excitement of discovering MacNeice in the appendix to the *Golden Treasury* at school, of just looking at them before attempting to understand the poems and seeing the words bloom on the page like the roses of 'Snow', waiting to unfold their meaning.

The look of words, the way they affect one another, the reactive colours of individual letters and numbers, the characters of characters have always fascinated me; the realization that rhyming was something that I could do came to me, when I was about three, by the pigpails of Pimlico, at a time when the postwar effort included feeding the nation's livestock: 'I'm not Ruth/ And that's the truth' was 'inspired' by a child from one of the neighbouring flats crossing the courtyard, and now the name Ruth still conjures up a little girl with dark pigtails (*pigtails* and *pigpails*) in a green and white gingham frock, as well as a colander full of potato peelings. *Colander* and *calendar*, and *fault*, a pale guilty tearful salt-stained word recalling our red Bakelite salt and pepper set, which was won at the fair on Hampstead Heath by the poets W.S. Graham and Tom Scott with whom we shared a rented house for a while, are examples of words inseparable from a childhood image imprinted at first awareness of them.

Sometimes just before falling asleep or when dozing after waking early, I watch a procession of wonderful jewels, flowers, fantastically plumaged birds, exotic animals, and speaking faces, beautiful, ordinary, evil: I can glimpse scenes from hell or hear heavenly music, operas or great choirs singing, or see a magnificent Gothic cathedral melt like candlewax, each one dissolving into the next; almost all irrecoverable except as a memory of marvellous colours and light, or corruption and horror. This is not a unique experience, and if, without the help of hallucinogens, we could enter at will that elusive cinema, what riches, what tales we could tell, but we have to make do with what the imagination can retrieve.

A story, by definition, requires a narrative, and it is in the narration that the hard labour of writing lies (writing lies); landscapes and still-lifes are easier, dialogue can be heard and tested in the head; the trick is to get them down on paper in a story worth telling. I am, however, reminded of the tragi-comic passage in Barrie's *Sentimental Tommy* wherein Tommy blows his chances in an essay competition (the Hugh Blackadder Mortification) by spending an hour searching for the perfect word, and brings ignominy on himself, his dominie and his school. Writing can be slow, and it is exhausting, because the writer is bringing a lifetime of experience to every sentence and each character, whether the created person is pure invention, an amalgam or even a private fictional tribute (q.v. 'Jane Austen's famous defence of the novel' in the *Oxford Dictionary of Quotations*, or *Northanger Abbey*).

Leaving aside the question of earning one's living (without referring to eye damage caused by the almost permanent wearing of reading glasses, or describing one's periodic emergences, blinking like a mole in the sunshine, to say not 'Hang spring cleaning!' but to echo MacNeice again:

> The shutter of time darkening ceaselessly
> Has whisked away the foam of may and elder
> And I realize how now, as every year before,
> Once again the gay months have eluded me.)

I avoid special pleading for those who are doing what they have chosen to do, and get great pleasure from it. It beats most other jobs, as I know very well, but the ability to work with words sometimes seems like a torment as well as a gift; I hesitate to say 'a poisoned chalice' lest I be tempted to get out Brewer. There are days when it is impossible to look at, say, a tree against the sky, without the brain insisting on translating every nuance into words, and recently, unwell and with a high temperature, I was tortured by this question: how do cats think without language? It is apparent that they do, but never in terms of Lemsip or something light on a tray, with a single rosebud in a vase and a freshly

ironed newspaper. Lost notebooks, lost chords – no sentence you can reconstruct will ever be quite as good as the original on some absconded scrap of paper – lost ideas that are just a tantalizing memory; there are days when all the world *is* paper and all the seas *are* ink ... was it 'hang' spring cleaning, or 'blow' spring cleaning? Time to search out *The Wind in the Willows*, whose faded green cover is such a good disguise, with my mother's handwriting evoking the past from its endpapers marbled in watered inks. Memories, ideas; there is much that I want, ought, or have been hired to write but meanwhile, what of those ten tiny silver-haired women in saris like moonstones, not one of them not more than four feet ten inches tall, whom I saw this morning at a bus stop? Who are they, where were they going, what is their story, and didn't Graham Greene write one about eight invisible Japanese gentlemen?

MY TURN

Sara Paretsky

Sartre writes he knew his mother existed to serve him. I
raised the two babies born when I was eight and thirteen
and cleaned the house every Saturday. I would have made
somebody a good old-fashioned kind of wife.

Sara Paretsky is the author of seven novels featuring female investigator, VI Warshawski. Her novel *Toxic Shock* won the Crime Writers' Association Silver Dagger for 1988. Her most recent publication is *Guardian Angel*.

MY TURN

At four the little girl's hair is a frizzy mass, a knot of tight curls around her head instead of the fine straight silk of other girls her age. Her mother makes one forlorn attempt to set it right, to put it in pincurls and smooth it out. But when the bobby pins come out, instead of the glossy curls the mother hoped for the daughter's frizz now stands up wildly all over her head.

'Witch! You're a witch!' Her older brother dances in a circle around her, pointing and doubling up in laughter.

The little girl scowls fiercely. 'I *am* a witch,' she says menacingly. 'And witches know everything.'

The brother's laughter collapses. He races to the kitchen, calling to his mother, 'Sara says she's a witch and witches know everything. She doesn't really know everything, does she?'

The mother soothes him and tells him of course not, that his sister was just making it up. That was my first story.

The Witch of the Seahouse lived in a beautiful stone house on a deserted beach. The water shimmered as if under moonlight even during the day. The Witch of the Seahouse used to come to me when I was very little, but afterwards she was replaced by the evil Witch of the Moon, who lived only in the dark, including the darkest part of my brain. After the day of my hair the Witch of the Seahouse never came back to me.

Soon after that my mother, weary of my unruly frizz and the tears at shampoo time, cut my hair close to my head. If I tried letting it grow out my father would mock me at dinner, telling me I looked like a sheepdog and to get it cut. I wore it short for many years, like my four brothers, like a fifth son.

In the stories I told in my head my hair was long and straight and glossy. In real life I was the Witch of the Moon, a monster. I struggled unsuccessfully for years to overcome the differences of appearance, of personality, of sex, that seemed to mark me as a monster both at home and in the world beyond.

It was only as I got older and began to absorb the example of my mother's cousin Agnes that I came to see myself differently. It took a long time to realize you could be independent, have a strong will, be a woman – and be human, not an evil witch. (And it wasn't until I read Woolf's 'Professions for Women' two years ago that I realized how universal the conflict between being angel and monster is for women who write.)

When I was little Agnes frightened me: she embodied too many strange qualities anathema to the world I lived in. I grew up in Kansas in the golden age of America, in a society where everyone had a defined place, where everyone knew right from wrong – and what happened when you forgot.

We had mandatory prayer (Protestant) in our public schools. The same schools barred blacks from college-track courses. In those golden days they knew better than to agitate about it. Abortion was a crime. Only bad girls had sex outside marriage – whereupon they reaped their inevitable punishment since such contraceptives as existed weren't available to unmarried women.

Best of all, we little girls knew we were destined to be mommies. We didn't worry about careers. Except for some married teachers the only women who worked were those too strange or too unfortunate to get husbands. And they were secretaries or waited tables in the coffee shops.

Our dreams were of our weddings. When Roxanne Farrell 'had to get married' in our sophomore year of high school, to us the most tawdry part was that she bought her trousseau at Woolworths. Good girls who waited until they graduated from high school or college bought fancy bridalwear at the Plaza in Kansas City.

Agnes – unmarried, travelling where and when she wanted (as I

write this she's seventy-one and trekking in Nepal), living not with a husband but a woman friend – was an embarrassment to be hidden from the neighbours.

Everything about her was labelled in red, danger, especially the fact that she was unmarried by choice. 'Who would want her?' my father demanded. 'She's too bossy – what man wants to be pushed around?'

With her friend Isabel she ran a girls' school, the first time I ever heard of a woman running her own business. Something about that made my father guffaw in a nasty way. 'Girls, of course she surrounds herself with girls. If she could get herself a real man she wouldn't be afraid of a few boys.'

My father had a way of saying things like that that made you feel you were an imbecile if you didn't know what he was talking about. We would whisper our questions – in case he treated them with contempt we could pretend we hadn't said anything.

'Why not?' I whispered now.

'The girls are irremediable,' said my mother, as if that was an answer. 'No one else can make them behave except Agnes.'

I still didn't understand, but knew better than to probe further.

When Agnes dropped in out of the blue – as she did from time to time on all her relatives – my father treated her with a nervous deference. It made me think she had great power – not only could she make irremediable girls behave but she even controlled him. My father terrified all of us, but in a way, her power over him frightened me even more: he would mock her behind her back but to her face, against his will, he was forced to obsequiousness.

Male writers such as Sartre and Bellow have recorded knowing early in life that their destiny lay in literature. Bellow knew he was 'born to be a performing and interpretive creature', Sartre that he was born for words.

I call myself a writer, but feebly, without conviction. Where did they get this sense, I wonder? Were their childhoods spent like mine? I wrote from an early age, but I knew that, as in all fields,

literature belonged to men. The history and biography we studied in school told tales of the deeds of men. We learned to speak of the aspirations of mankind and of 'man's inhumanity to man' – his inhumanity to woman not being worth recording.

And the literature we studied was all written by men. If they were like me, Bellow and Sartre may not even have known that women wrote in a serious way, that the first novelist to treat psychology as a significant force in human lives was a woman. Sartre's boyhood was spent with Flaubert, Cornelius, Homer, Shakespeare. Bellow went to Anderson, Dreiser, Edgar Lee Masters, Vachel Lindsay.

The books Sartre's grandmother read were feminine, he says, and he was taught by his grandfather to deem them inferior. By an odd chance I was taught the same lesson. We studied only one novel by a woman in my school – and her first name was George. Although I wept over *Little Women*, the moral of Jo March's life is that little girls must put aside the dream of literature to perform the higher duty of looking after their families.

Did their childhoods resemble mine in other ways? Was Jean-Paul or Saul's first responsibility to look after the little children – to spend summer vacation and evenings after school taking them for walks, changing their diapers, feeding them, reading them their stories? Did their fathers tell them their works were derivative, that they lacked the genius necessary for originality? Did their mothers assure them that the work their sisters did was superior to anything they could ever do, that the future lies with girls, not boys? Can destiny swim in such waters?

All my childhood dreams were directed to the present, specifically to escaping it, until I learned escape wasn't possible. My older brother and I would look at a picture of a ship at sea or a beautiful island, some strange wonderful place we wished to be. We would hold hands and run toward the picture, and by wishing hard enough be transported into it. More often we climbed on to the two hitching posts in front of our house – remnants of the days when visitors had horses to tie up. After turning around

three times we jumped, landing in a magic world where we fought dragons and loving elves came to our rescue.

The walls of my bedroom were papered with cabbage roses and behind the roses lay a corridor, a long hall whose windows looked on perpetual sunlight. After going to bed I could get into this corridor and live a life of total secrecy.

When I was eight my mother had a baby. While she was pregnant I dreamed of having a sister, but she produced another boy to go with the two she already had. She put the baby in my room and told me to look after him.

I had longed for a doll that cried real tears – I'd seen one at Grand Central Station when we moved from New York to Kansas and had always wished for one. They gave me my brother and said I would like him much better than a doll. In fact, they gave him my dolls to break, since I was now too grown up to want them. Getting a baby to look after ended my magic worlds. In my stories I was still a princess but I knew now they were stories and would never come true.

When I was seven my mother stood me on a chair next to the kitchen counter and had me bake a cake and cookies for my father and brothers, beginning a weekly baking stint that lasted until I left their house at seventeen.

Sartre writes he knew his mother existed to serve him. I raised the two babies born when I was eight and thirteen and cleaned the house every Saturday. I would have made somebody a good old-fashioned kind of wife. It wasn't that I fought my destiny – it just somehow side-stepped me.

Maybe my hair saved me, cropped close to my head when everyone else wore hers long – it made me look too strange. Or maybe it was my stories – I wanted a man from one of my stories, not the pimply, self-absorbed ones who came to dorm mixers. Or maybe it was a message absorbed from Agnes – against my will at first, then later with great eagerness.

The summer I turned ten, on one of her abrupt visits, Agnes learned I was writing a story. She asked me to read it to her. She

sat in the living room and listened with total attention. It still seems unbelievable to me that a grown woman could really *want* to spend an hour hearing a young girl read a story. She didn't offer any literary criticism. I don't even remember her saying anything. Just that she sat and listened.

Sartre records how his mother used to go into transports over his writing, showing his boyish 'novels' to neighbours and to her father, with whom they lived. She would stand over his shoulder while he wrote, in ecstasies over his imagination. It was one of her intimates who named writing as young Jean-Paul's career when he was seven or eight. His cousins were told they would be engineers.

Both of my parents had stories to tell, their sides, in an unending feud, and both would make use of my writing to help them make their points – my mother wanting me to write poems describing her entrapment, my father, stories proclaiming his unlauded glories. But beyond that my words created so little interest that my mother tells me my father burned all my childhood papers in some housekeeping frenzy or other. I keep hoping she got it wrong. I spend hours feverishly hunting through her attic for some story, some diary, a remnant that will connect me with my past, that may tell me what dreams I used to have. Nothing comes to light. Despite my anguish I'm relieved that the forced bondage of my words to my parents has also vanished.

Agnes's listening to one story was not enough to give me a sense that my future lay in words. It was enough, though, to keep me writing.

After Agnes listened to my story I would lie in bed imagining my parents dead and me adopted by her, taken into her school where there were only girls.

The dream took on new dimensions the following year when we moved to a house in the country five miles from the town of Lawrence. At first I loved it: I finally had my own room and we went to a two-room country school – just like in *Understood Betsy* or *On the Banks of Plum Creek*. Later I came to hate it. My

parents' fights intensified and the isolation of the country made it easy to seal me off completely from friends my own age, from any activities but school and housework.

The main line of the Santa Fe crossed the road at the bottom of the hill on the outskirts of Lawrence. There wasn't any crossing gate or bell and every now and then the Kansas City Chief, roaring around a blind curve toward San Francisco, would annihilate a family.

Mary and Dave would be arguing, not paying attention to the road or to the tracks. The crash would be appalling. We'd be at the house, of course, my four brothers and I, lounging around reading or maybe playing softball. We should have been doing a dozen chores – mowing the lawn (my older brother's job), vacuuming (mine), changing the baby's diapers (mine again) or sorting the bottles out of the trash to take to the dump (my brother). 'I don't need a dishwasher,' Mary used to tell visitors, 'I have two right here.' And she would point at my older brother and me.

When we heard the car in the drive we leaped into action, attacking our chores – there was hell to pay if we were found loafing in bourgeois self-indulgence. And then we saw it was the sheriff's car, the red light flashing. We raced over to see what he wanted, me grabbing the baby and carrying him along on my hip.

The sheriff looked at us very kindly. He said maybe we should go sit down. He had something very serious to tell us. There'd been an accident and we were orphans now. Was there someone we could call to look after us? Of course not, we already did any looking after there was to do, but we couldn't tell him that, and anyway, of course, we were underage, we needed guardians.

I would go to Agnes, to the school for irremediable girls. Even though she only took girls I would have to bring the two little boys with me, they were mine to look after (they thought I was their mother. When they started kindergarten they didn't know what 'sister' meant – they didn't know that was me: they thought they had two mothers.) I didn't care where the other two went, they could look after themselves.

We looked solemnly at the sheriff, conjuring up tears out of shock, but we couldn't believe it had really happened: we were really orphans. Just like *Anne of Green Gables* or *English Orphans*. Our future changed miraculously.

And then Mary and Dave would come up the drive, still arguing, not dead at all, and we would leap into activity that was never quite frenzied enough. My older brother could never get tasks quite right, or the tasks set for him would change between when they were assigned and when he did them, and most of the yelling went his way. The rest of us slid upstairs.

Agnes didn't come to see us again after the summer she heard me read. Maybe she grew too busy, or maybe the number of fights in our house and their ferocity drove her away. I don't know. Maybe it was simply her paying so much attention to me – it might have frightened my father into telling her she couldn't come again.

He thought she was a lesbian, of course, although I only realized that later. WOMAN ON THE LOOSE! WEIRD WOMAN OUT OF CONTROL! That was the headline on my father's face when he talked about Agnes. It was out of the question for me to live with her – he wasn't going to risk losing control of me.

I've never known if she was a lesbian or not, even when I came to spend more time with her: it's never seemed particularly important. One thing I found out about Agnes was that her mother died when she was ten, died giving birth to a baby that didn't survive long, either. Agnes was named for her mother, who gave her her wedding ring as a memento when she knew she was dying. I don't know how that affected Agnes, but it would have frightened me out of marriage. (When I got married she insisted I take her mother's ring. I'm still not sure if that gift portends good or ill; just in case, I never wear it.)

Agnes took a more active role in my life after I moved to Chicago. She appeared to me suddenly, a *dea ex machina*, during my first winter there. Although she didn't stay there long, Chicago

is where she ran to when she was twenty, away from the care of a family that took more than they gave. She might have come to see me, looking for her younger self.

I was twenty-one then, fat, ungainly. I'd never had a boyfriend and, aside from my three room-mates, I didn't have many women friends in Chicago, either. My room-mates and I shared a dismal apartment on the south side – six rooms for a hundred and sixty-five dollars a month and all the cockroaches we could eat. We killed two hundred and fifty of them one night, spraying the oven where they nested and stomping on them when they scampered out. You'd have to be twenty-one to want to count the bodies.

It was never warmer than fifty-five in the building and that was a most bitter winter. The city code says it has to be at least sixty-two during the day. We'd get building inspectors out who would solemnly measure the air. Then they'd learn the landlady worked as a precinct captain for the Daley machine and their thermometer miraculously would register fifteen degrees higher than ours.

I had gone to Kansas for the Christmas holidays and was back several days before my room-mates. Carrying my heavy suitcase up the stairs to the apartment entrance I blundered into the doorjamb, knocking the wind out of myself. I dumped my suitcase down and sat on it, not even going inside, so miserable with my fat, my clumsiness, my loneliness that I hoped I might just die right there.

My two youngest brothers would care, of course, as would my friend Kathleen, but my parents wouldn't even come to the funeral. I'd been active in community organizing both in Chicago and Lawrence; admiring community leaders came to the service to pay me homage. In my coffin I looked like a Botticelli angel, miraculously slender with long soft golden curls. The picture moved me to tears.

'What's wrong with you?' It was Agnes. I hadn't seen her come into the unlit stairwell.

I was so startled that I lost my balance and fell to the floor with a crash of suitcase and legs. 'Nothing,' I muttered. 'I didn't know you were going to be here.'

I was terrified I'd been told and had forgotten – during this very low point in my life people were always telling me things that I didn't seem to hear.

'Neither did I. I called Mary to get your phone number and she told me you were just getting back to town today. Sorry if I frightened you.'

I got back to my feet somehow and unlocked the apartment door. Just navigating the strip from the hall to the living room was an agony – I ran into the jamb once more and was so nervous that I tripped over the suitcase. Agnes made no comment then or later on my shambling, awkward gait, nor on the freezing apartment which stank of mould and Raid.

She took me out to dinner, just her – Isabel hadn't come on this particular trip – and made me feel alert, witty, intelligent. She assumed I had an adult understanding of people – from the waiters to the US Congress to my own parents – and I responded with what seemed to me to be enormous sophistication. Late in the evening she told me I had beautiful hands and should plan to do something fine with them, and to this day, in the disgust I can't overcome for my body, I look at my hands with a loverlike admiration.

After that I used to visit her and Isabel. In those days you could fly on student-standby for some trivial price and I'd go in the summer and during the Christmas holidays. She didn't run the school any more. In the wake of Title VII legislation she'd been asked to take a role in shaping education policy. And she thought perhaps the country was changing in some way that would make it easier for little girls, that they wouldn't need special schools any more. Now she's not so sure, but in that era we all had heady dreams.

I've never stopped walking into doorjambs, but Agnes trained me to do it with my head up, without apologizing. She and Isabel taught me some of the basics that I'd never gotten the hang of, such as how to feel at better ease inside my own body. As a teenager I'd tied down my breasts, ashamed of their betrayal,

their announcement that I was a girl. Agnes taught me, if not to love them, at least to live with them. Most of all she and Isabel taught me how to listen when other people talked, by listening to me with interest.

Agnes didn't ask about my stories and I was too uncertain about them to remind her of the day she'd listened ten years before. I kept thinking I should go to medical school, become a surgeon to justify her faith in my hands. Or perhaps a painter, but painting is such a public art. You can write a story and no one will know you've done it, but when you paint a picture it's apparent that you've been doing something, even if you only keep it in the privacy of your home.

A few years later I finally showed Agnes one of my stories because I couldn't explain in any other way the lives of some people I cared about, yet who troubled me. She was amazed – she didn't know I still wrote – she thought my academic work had taken that place in my life. She praised my writing and made me feel it might be something fine, like my hands. She urged me to try to publish my tale and told me about the burgeoning feminist magazines that nurtured women's art. I sent my story out and *Women: A Journal of Liberation* accepted it.

I'd published one other story, when I was eleven, in the *American Girl*. They had a section called 'My Turn' for contributions by readers. My entry was a story but they printed it as non-fiction, an uneasy sign to me that it wouldn't have made the grade if they'd known it was original, creative. Until Agnes urged me I never tried sending any of my other writing to publishers.

After *A Journal of Liberation* published my story, the romance I wove in my head was that I would write a book, a novel, and that it would be published. It took six more years before I was strong enough to make that dream happen. It was then that I started work on my first book, *Indemnity Only*.

I haven't seen Agnes for some time now, since 1982 when she came to celebrate the publication of *Indemnity Only*. Although I still hear from Isabel I find it painful that Agnes thinks I no longer need her.

For me the hardest part of telling stories is crossing the line from private words to public ones. When I write for myself alone the words come freely, but when I know someone else will read them they're like water squeezed from a stone. I think I still need Agnes, to give me more confidence in my voice, but she's spending her time with other irremediable girls whose troubles seem more serious – not running her school again, but seeking them out as she sought me.

Still, I've finally let my hair grow out. I've even learned to like my wild frizz. It gives me some assurance that I, too, may yet come to be a wild woman, not under anyone's control.

I've written five novels, all of them featuring a woman named VI Warshawski, a detective who lives alone but whose close friend is a doctor some twenty years her senior named Lotty Herschel. People sometimes ask if VI is me, if Lotty is based on someone real. They're not: you can't put real people in a book, at least I can't – if I try to describe a real person's idiosyncrasies and make a fictional character act the way that a real person would, everything becomes wooden. The action can't flow naturally because my imagination is penned in by how that living person would have acted.

But VI and Lotty are real, of course, because the only basis for imagining people is people. Even if VI isn't me, Lotty isn't Agnes, their relationship is real. Everyone needs an Agnes so that she can find her own voice, so that her stories don't die in her head.

THE DEVIL FINDS WORK FOR IDLE HANDS

John McGahern

There are no days more full in childhood than those days that were not lived at all, the days lost in a favourite book ... Nowadays, only when I am writing am I able to find again that complete absorption when all sense of time is lost, maybe once in a year or two. It is a strange and complete kind of happiness ...

John McGahern is the distinguished novelist and short-story writer whose second novel, *The Dark*, was banned in his native Ireland. His works include *The Pornographer* and *High Ground*. His most recent novel, *Amongst Women*, was short-listed for the Booker Prize and won the GPA Prize.

THE DEVIL FINDS WORK FOR IDLE HANDS

I came to write through reading. It is such an obvious path that I hesitate to state it, but so much confusion now surrounds the artistic act that the simple and the obvious may be in need of statement. I think reading and writing are as close as they are separate. In my case, I came to read through pure luck. I had great good fortune when I was ten or eleven. I was given the run of a library. I believe it changed my life and without it I would never have become a writer.

There were few books in our house, and reading for pleasure was not approved of. It was thought to be dangerous, like pure laughter. In the emerging class in the Ireland of the 1940s, when an insecure sectarian state was being guided by a philistine church, the stolidity of a long empty grave face was thought to be the height of decorum and profundity. 'The devil always finds work for idle hands,' was one of the warning catch-phrases. Time was filled by necessary work, always exaggerated: sleep, Gaelic football, prayer, gossip, religious observance, the giving of advice – ponderously delivered, and received in stupor – civil war politics, and the eternal busyness that Proust describes as Moral Idleness. This was confined mostly to the new emerging classes – civil servants, policemen, doctors, teachers, tillage inspectors. The ordinary farming people went about their sensible pagan lives as they had done for centuries, seeing all this as one of the many veneers they had to pretend to wear, like all the others they had worn since the time of the Druids.

During this time I was given the free run of Moroney's library. They were Protestants. Old Willie Moroney lived with his son,

Andy, in their two-storied stone house, which was surrounded by a huge orchard and handsome stone outhouses. Willie must have been well into his eighties then, and Andy was about forty. Their natures were so stress-free that it is no wonder they were both to live into their nineties. Old Willie, the beekeeper, with his great beard and fondness for St Ambrose and Plato, 'the Athenian bee, the good and the wise ... because his words glowed with the sweetness of honey', is wonderfully brought to life in David Thomson's *Woodbrook*. Willie had not gone upstairs since his wife's death, nor had he washed, and he lived in royal untidiness in what had once been the dining room, directly across the stone hallway from the library, that dear hallway with its barometer and antlered coatrack, and the huge silent clock. The front door, with its small brass plate shaped into the stone for the doorbell, was never opened. All access to the house was by the back door, up steps from the farmyard, and through the littered kitchen to the hallway and stairs and front rooms. David Thomson describes the Moroneys as landless, which is untrue, for they owned a hundred-and-seventy acres of the sweetest land on the lower plains of Boyle, itself some of the best limestone land in all of Ireland. The farm was beautifully enclosed by roads which ran from the high demesne wall of Rockingham to the broken walls of Oakport. The Moroneys should have been wealthy. They had to have money to build that stone house in the first place, to build and slate the stone houses that enclosed the farmyard, to acquire the hundreds of books that lined the walls of the library: David Thomson, though, is right in spirit, for Willie and Andy had all the appearance of being landless. Most of Andy's time was taken up with the study of astronomy. Willie lived for his bees. He kept the hives at the foot of the great orchard. They both gathered apples, stored them on wooden shelves in the first of the stone houses of the farmyard, and they sold them by the bucketful, and seemed glad enough for the half-crowns they received. As a boy, I was sent to buy apples, somehow fell into conversation with Willie about books, and was given the run of the library. There

was Scott, Dickens, Meredith and Shakespeare, books by Zane Grey and Jeffery Farnol, and many, many books about the Rocky Mountains. Some person in that nineteenth-century house must have been fascinated by the Rocky Mountains. I didn't differentiate, I read for nothing but pleasure, the way a boy nowadays might watch endless television dramas. Every week or fortnight, for years, I'd return with five or six books in my oilcloth shopping bag and take five or six away. Nobody gave me direction or advice. There was a tall slender ladder for getting to books on the high shelves. Often, in the incredibly cluttered kitchen, old Willie would ask me about the books over tea and bread. I think it was more out of the need for company than any real curiosity.

I remember one such morning vividly. We were discussing a book I had returned and drinking tea with bread and jam. All I remember about that particular book was that it was large and flat and contained coloured illustrations, of plants and flowers probably, and these would have interested Willie because of the bees. The morning was one of those still true mornings in summer before the heat comes, the door open on the yard. Earlier that morning he must have gone through his hives – the long grey beard was stained with food and drink and covered his shirt front – and while he was talking some jam fell into the beard and set off an immediate buzzing. Without interrupting the flow of his talk, he shambled to the door, extracted the two or three errant bees caught in the beard, and flung them into the air of the yard.

I continued coming to the house for books after the old bee-keeper's death, but there was no longer any talk of books. Andy developed an interest in the land, but, I fear, it was as impractical as astronomy. Because of my constant presence about the house, I was drawn into some of those ventures, but their telling has no place here.

I have often wondered why no curb was put on my reading at home. I can only put it down to a prejudice in favour of the gentle, eccentric Moroneys, and Protestants in general. At the time, Protestants were pitied because they were bound for hell in

the next world, and they were considered to be abstemious, honest, and morally more correct than the general run of our fellow Catholics. The prejudice may well have extended to their library. The books may have been thought to be as harmless as their gentle owners. For whatever reason, the books were rarely questioned, and as long as they didn't take from work or prayer I was allowed to read without hindrance.

There are no days more full in childhood than those days that were not lived at all, the days lost in a favourite book. I remember waking out of one such book in the middle of the large living room in the barracks, to find myself surrounded. My sisters had unlaced and removed one of my shoes and placed a straw hat on my head. Only when they began to move the wooden chair on which I sat away from the window did I wake out of the book – to their great merriment. Nowadays, only when I am writing am I able to find again that complete absorption when all sense of time is lost, maybe once in a year or two. It is a strange and complete kind of happiness, of looking up from the pages, thinking it is still nine or ten in the morning, to discover that it is past lunchtime; and there is no longer anyone who will test the quality of the absence by unlacing and removing a shoe.

Sometimes I have wondered if it would have made any difference if my reading had been guided or structured, but there is no telling such things in an only life. Pleasure is by no means an infallible, critical guide, W. H. Auden wrote; but it is the least fallible. That library and those two gentle men were, to me, a pure blessing.

A time comes when the way we read has to change drastically or stop, though it may well continue as an indolence or drug. This change is linked with our growing consciousness, consciousness that we will not live forever and that all human life is essentially in the same fix. We have to discard all the tenets that we have been told until we have succeeded in thinking them out for ourselves. We find that we are no longer reading books for the story and that all stories are more or less the same story; and we

begin to come on certain books that act like mirrors. What they reflect is something dangerously close to our own life and the society in which we live. A new, painful excitement enters the way we read. We search out these books, and these books only, the books that act as mirrors. The quality of the writing becomes more important than the quality of the material out of which the pattern or story is shaped. We find that we can no longer read certain books that once we could not put down; other books that previously were tedious take on a completely new excitement and meaning: even the Rocky Mountains has to become an everywhere, like *Mansfield Park*, if it is to retain our old affection.

That change happened to me in the Dublin of the 1950s. Again, I think I was lucky. There were many good secondhand bookshops in which one could root about for hours. One book barrow in particular, on a corner of Henry Street, was amazing. Most of the books found there then would now be described as modern classics. How the extraordinary Mr Kelly acquired them we never asked. These were times when books were discussed in dance halls as well as in bars. It was easy then to get a desk in the National Library. The staff were kind and would even bring rare books on request. There were inexpensive seats at the back of the Gate Theatre, and there were many pocket theatres, often in Georgian basements. Out in Dun Laoghaire there was the Gas Company Theatre where we had to walk trough the silent show-room of gas cookers to get to see Pirandello or Chekhov or Lorca or Tennessee Williams. The city was full of cinemas. I remember seeing *Julius Caesar* with Gielgud and Brando, playing to full houses in the Metropole. At weekends, cinema tickets were sold on the black market. One such black marketeer, a pretty girl I knew, showed me a fistful of unsold tickets one wet Sunday night shortly before eight o'clock and said, 'If I don't get rid of some of these soon – and at bloody cost at that – I'll have to let down me drawers before the night is out.' And there was the tiny Astor on the quays where I first saw *Casque d'Or*, *Rules of the Game*, and *Children of Paradise*.

Much has been written about the collusion of church and state to bring about an Irish society that was insular, repressive, and sectarian. This is partly true, but because of the long emphasis on the local and the individual in a society that never found any true cohesion, it was only superficially successful.

I think that women fared worst of all within this paternalistic mishmash, but to men with intellectual interests it had at the time, I believe, some advantage. Granted, we were young and had very little to lose, but the system was so blatantly foolish in so many of its manifestations that it could only provoke the defence of laughter, though never, then, in public. What developed was a freemasonry of the intellect with a vigorous underground life of its own that paid scant regard to church or state. Even an obscene book, we would argue, could not be immoral if it was truly written. Most of the books that were banned, like most books published, were not worth reading, and those that were worth reading could be easily found and quickly passed around. There is no taste so sharp as that of forbidden fruit. This climate also served to cut out a lot of the pious humbug that often afflicts the arts. Literature was not considered 'good'. There was no easy profit. People who need to read, who need to think and see, will always find a way around a foolish system, and difficulty will only make that instinct stronger, as it serves in another sphere to increase desire. In no way can this clownish system be recommended wholeheartedly, but it was the way it was and we were young and socially unambitious and we managed. The more we read of other literatures, and the more they were discussed, the more clearly it emerged that not only was Yeats a very great poet but that almost singlehandedly he had, amazingly, laid down a whole framework in which an indigenous literature could establish traditions and grow. His proud words, 'The knowledge of reality is a secret knowledge; it is a kind of death,' was for us, socially as well as metaphorically, true.

The two living writers who meant most to us were Samuel Beckett and Patrick Kavanagh. They belonged to no establishment,

and some of their best work was appearing in the little magazines that could be found at the Eblana Bookshop on Grafton Street. Beckett was in Paris. The large-hatted figure of Kavanagh was an inescapable sight around Grafton Street, his hands often clasped behind his back, muttering hoarsely to himself as he passed. Both, through their work, were living, exciting presences in the city. I wish I could open a magazine now with the same excitement with which I once opened *Nimbus*: 'Ignore Power's schismatic sect,/ Lovers alone lovers protect'. (The same poet could also rhyme *catharsis* with *arses*, but even his wild swing was like no other.)

When I began to write – and it was in those Dublin years – it was without any thought of publication. In many ways, it was an extension of reading as well as a kind of play. Words had been physical presences for me for a long time before, each word with its own weight, colour, shape, relationship, extending out into a world without end. Change any word in a single sentence and immediately all the other words demand to be rearranged. By writing and rewriting sentences, by moving their words endlessly around, I found that scenes or pictures and echoes and shapes began to emerge that obscurely reflected a world that had found its first expression and recognition through reading. I don't know how long that first excitement lasted – for a few years, I think – before it changed to work, though that first sense of play never quite goes away and, in all the most important ways, a writer remains a beginner throughout his working life. Now I find I will resort to almost any subterfuge to escape the blank page, but there seems to be always some scene or rhythm that lodges in the mind and will not go away until written down. Often when they are written down it turns out that there was never anything real behind the rhythm or scene, and they disappear in the writing; other times those scenes or rhythms start to grow, and you find yourself once again working every day, sometimes over a period of several years, to discover and bring to life a world through words as if it were the first and (this is ever a devout prayer) last time. It is true that there can be times of intense happiness

throughout the work, when all the words seem, magically, to find their true place, and several hours turn into a single moment; but these occurrences are so rare that they are, I suspect, like mirages in desert fables, to encourage and torment the half-deluded traveller.

Like gold in the ground or the alchemist's mind it is probably wise not to speak about the pursuit at all. Technique can certainly be learned, and only a fool would try to do without it, but technique for its own sake grows heartless. Unless technique can take us to that clear mirror that is called style – the reflection of personality in language, everything having been removed from it that is not itself – then the most perfect technique is as worthless as mere egotism. Once work reaches that clearness the writer's task is ended. His or her words will not live again until and unless they find their true reader.

John Banville

Fictional characters are made of words, not flesh; they do not have free will, they do not exercise volition. They are easily born, and as easily killed off. They have their flickering lives, and die on cue, for us, giving up their little paragraph of pathos.

John Banville is an award-winning novelist with a richly gothic style and a metaphysical vein. His novels include *Mefisto* and *The Newton Letter*. His novel *The Book of Evidence* won the GPA Award and was short-listed for the Booker Prize. His most recent novel is *Ghosts*.

I do not think I am a novelist. As a writer I have little or no interest in character, plot, motivation, manners, politics, morality, social issues. The word *psychology* when it is applied to art makes me want to reach for my revolver. To those of you who at this point are about to stop reading, let me hasten to say that this is not an anti-humanist attitude I am striking, nor even, really, a postmodernist one. I do believe that the art of fiction does deal with the world, that world which in our arrogance we call 'ordinary', but that it deals with it in very special and specialized ways. I am enough of a deconstructionist to acknowledge that the novelist's intentions for his novel may in the end not count for as much as he imagined or desired that they would. Frequently it happens that a novel will live on into posterity – a rare phenomenon, I grant – because of qualities which for the author were secondary, or of which at the time of writing perhaps he was not even aware. In saying this, however, I do not mean to agree with those critics – and they are by no means only the most advanced ones: read the fiction reviews in the Sunday supplements – who look on the novelist as a dead hand which performs a kind of automatic writing. Novelists themselves contribute to this misconception of what they do and how they do it. When I hear a writer talking earnestly of how the characters in his latest book 'took over the action' I am inclined to laugh (or, if I am in a good mood, acknowledge a colleague doing his best to get through yet another interview). Fictional characters are made of words, not flesh; they do not have free will, they do not exercise volition. They are easily born, and as easily killed off. They have their

flickering lives, and die on cue, for us, giving up their little paragraph of pathos. They are at once less and more than what they seem.

The writers I most admire are the ones who have abandoned the pretence of realism, who have ceased to try to speak about things in favour of speaking the things themselves, such as Beckett, or Thomas Bernhard, or those who took the old forms and worked a revolution from within, such as Henry James, or, well, Henry James. The wrought and polished object itself, an astonishment standing in the world – a jar in Tennessee! – that is what interests me. The world and being in it are such a mystery that the artist stands before it in a trance of bafflement, like an idiot at High Mass. In confrontation with the total enigma, all that the artist can do, it seems to me, is set up analogues, parallel microcosms, tiny models of the huge original with which the mind may play in earnest. I am speaking of a pictured world, not a world anatomized. Nietzsche was the first to recognize that the true depth of a thing is in its surface. Art is shallow, and therein lie its deeps. The face is all, and, in front of the face, the mask.

By what means, then, does fiction *get at* the world? Not by engagement, I am convinced, but precisely by disengagement, by adopting a posture of bland innocence, standing back with empty palms on show. Listen, the writer says, listen – here is the music of things as they are, changed upon the blue guitar. The subject matter hardly matters. Flaubert is wondered at and excoriated in equal measure for his stated wish to write a book that would be *about nothing*, but he was merely acknowledging the fact, unpalatable to many, that all art aspires to the condition of pure style. 'In literature,' says Henry James, 'we move through a blest world in which we know nothing except by style, but in which also everything is saved by it.' I believe, with Hermann Broch, that art is, or should be, a mode of objective knowledge of the world, not an expression of the subjective world. As Kafka momentously said, the artist is the man who has nothing to say.

*

JOHN BANVILLE

First comes, for me, the shape. Before I put down even a note for a novel, there exists in my mind, or just outside it somewhere, a figure, not geometrical, exactly, not like something out of Euclid, more a sort of self-sustaining tension in space, tangible yet wholly imaginary, which represents, which in some sense *is*, the completed thing. The task is to bring this figure out of the space of the potential and into the world, where it will be manifest yet hidden, like the skeleton beneath the skin.

At an essential level, therefore, the work of art is for me no more and no less than the solution – partial, always, of course – to a technical problem. The problem is that of placing certain figures on a certain ground so that they shall seem to move, and breathe, and have their lives. How is it to be done? Will it seem paradoxical, in the light of what I have said so far, if I now insist that the only way to portray life in art is to be as lifelike as possible? All that the writer has to work with is human being, his own and that of the mysterious others, what little he can know of it, of them. Even the most abstract art is grounded in the mundane, composed, like us, of Eros and of dust. Life will keep breaking in. However, 'life' here means life in its *appearance*, that is, both in the way it looks, and in the way it makes itself manifest in the world. The phenomenological breath that wafts from that sentence makes me think that the word I should be using in this context is not *life*, but *being*, or even – I whisper it – Being.

The novel, since it is an organic growth, generates, or should, its own rules, which will govern every smallest ramification of its form and content. The novel grows by a process of genetic building, filling itself out, matching itself to its vision of itself, as a tree grows, becoming a tree by becoming a tree. To break the rules of generation is to break the book. Of course, the novelist can make mistakes, and will, since he is human. Randall Jarrell defined the novel as an extended work of prose fiction which has something wrong with it. There are critics who contend that the being wrong – that is, being defective in form, loose in content, ragged in style – is a large part of the novel's strength, that its

imperfections make it sturdy and vigorous and lifelike. As Frank Kermode has pointed out, we seek in art a completedness, a 'sense of an ending', not available to us in life (who remembers his own birth, who will know his own death? – all we have is the drifting moment), and, yes, I suppose the truest art will be that which refuses us the neatness of the finished thing. But there is wrong and wrong (there is true and true, also, but that is another matter). Human endeavour can always be counted on for inbuilt flaws, for infelicities of tone and clumsiness of execution. It is when the rules, the deep grammar, of the work of art are bent or broken that the internal structure crumbles. In the novel, such transgressions are more easily detected, I think, than in other forms of art, precisely because the novel is the most lifelike form there is.

Is it not a curious thing, this true-to-lifeness that fiction manages? Albert Einstein was always fascinated, and made not a little uneasy, by the weird way in which physical reality conforms so neatly to the manmade discipline of mathematics. It is hardly less strange that a progression of dark marks on a light surface should cause an eerily persuasive version of the quotidian world to blossom in the brain of the reader sitting under the lamplight with his book, forgetful of himself and of his surroundings. What magic is it that makes us think we are sailing on the Pequod, that we are a little in love with Isabel Archer, that we see the streets of Dublin on a summer day in 1904 through the eyes of Leopold Bloom? How is it that a made-up story should seem to utter that which Wallace Stevens's Large Red Man reads aloud out of the purple tabulae, 'The outlines of being and its expressings, the syllables of its law'? Fiction is a kind of infinitesimal calculus, approaching nearer and ever nearer to life itself and yet never really having anything of real life in it at all, except the fictionist's obsessive and doomed determination to *get it right* (if that really is a human desideratum). Or am I giving too much weight to the merely real?

This is Wallace Stevens again:

'Credences of Summer'

The personae of summer play the characters
Of an inhuman author, who meditates
With the gold bugs, in blue meadows, late at night.
He does not hear his characters talk. He sees
Them mottled, in the moodiest costumes

Of blue and yellow, sky and sun, belted
And knotted, sashed and seamed, half pales of red,
Half pales of green, appropriate habit for
The huge decorum, the manner of the time,
Part of the mottled mood of summer's whole,

In which the characters speak because they want
To speak, the fat, the roseate characters,
Free, for a moment, from malice and sudden cry,
Complete in a completed scene, speaking
Their parts as in a youthful happiness.

As always with Stevens, I am not sure that I know what it is he is talking about here, but I find the passage strangely affecting, and hear in it a description of sorts of what it is I do when I come to write fiction. The fat, the roseate characters move as in a moving scene, in this little glass untouchable theatre of the mind. If they are lifelike it is because so much of life is missing from them and their doings, the dross which is true life itself thrown out in obedience to the laws of a necessary economy. Fledgling novelists are forever worrying about the furniture (how will I get these characters into bed? – how, for God's sake, will I even get them up the stairs and through the bedroom door?); it takes a long time for the apprentice to realize that action in a novel is not a matter of stage management but of artistic concentration. Under the artist's humid scrutiny the object grows warm, it stirs and shies, giving off the blush of verisimilitude; the flash of his

relentless gaze strikes them and the little monsters rise and walk, their bandages unfurling. The world they inhabit is a world of words, and yet, as with Josefine the mouse singer's piping song, 'something of our poor brief childhood is in it, something of a lost happiness that can never be found again, but it also has something of our busy life here and now, of that little admixture of unfathomable gaiety which persists and cannot be extinguished'.

I do not know how it is done.

Is it magic or mere sleight of hand?

(Mere?)

HEADY STUFF

Susan Hill

I have sometimes stood in front of a novel to be written, and it has been like a mountain, I have said, 'Oh no, no, this time you have gone too far . . .' But inside, with glee, I knew I was lying, that I could not, yet ultimately, I could pretend that I could, and so I would, and did.

Susan Hill is the author of ten novels, whose work has been translated into sixteen languages. In 1972 she won the Whitbread Prize for her novel, *Bird of Night*. Her 1973 novel, *Woman in Black*, was adapted for the West End stage. Her most recent novel is *Mist in the Mirror*. She is currently at work on a sequel to Daphne Du Maurier's *Rebecca*.

HEADY STUFF

There are some questions to be got out of the way. Those, for instance, to do with texts asked very often by students, in long questionnaires, and sometimes in person. There they sit before me, in flesh or in spirit, notebooks ready, pens poised, texts open, well-thumbed, well marked-up, expectant – and why not? Of course they expect me to know all the answers, who better, and to sort them out definitively – this, this and this are so, that is not, I meant X to be a symbol of such and such, it happens this way because – after all, I wrote the thing, who else knows the whole truth about it if not the author, so they've got a head start, haven't they, as I'm there to answer their questions, they've stolen a march on the other candidates, they have it from the horse's mouth. What is the meaning of this, why did you, why, why, why? Answers full but clear, and as neatly digested as possible please. Ah, if only it were that simple, if only. I mean it, I would love to be able to help you, solve all your problems, answer everything with absolute authority, get you all A's. But you each read the books individually, and they become a part of you and your own inner imaginations, you may read all manner of things into them, may find all sorts of symbols and resonances and parallels, and have answers which are perfectly valid for you, even though I did not know these things were there, I did not consciously put them into the books, I cannot tell you whether or not you are right, for in these grey, infinitely variable areas, there is no absolute right, save in certain banal and entirely superficial areas. I can reply to those questions well enough but those are not the interesting or important ones, let alone the ones you need help

with. Still, at least I can perhaps point you in the right direction, disabuse you of some of your teacher's dottier notions which have been presented to you as gospel.

There are other questions easily dealt with. The boring, familiar ones. Do you use a word processor? Really, you actually still write with a pen (the word 'quill' hovers in the air)? Do you write every day or do you wait for inspiration? How do I get my novel published?

No, no, these are not the questions that are only very occasionally tentatively asked, but which haunt my own sleeping and waking more and more, in a way they never did. I never used to address them, never would have thought they mattered. But when one is young, one never seriously addresses the question of death, either. And the two are related, they matter almost as much, I find.

Why, why, why? Why write? Why fiction? When I began, all those years ago, when I was young, brash and indecently full of confidence, when I took and cleared hurdles I did not even see were there, I never asked why. Do any of us? We take it for granted. And so we should. I breathe because I do and cannot not, and still live. I write, ditto.

I don't remember learning to read, early readers rarely do. But I remember, just, not being able to. My father had the *Yorkshire Post* open, in front of his face for ages, hours it seemed, he read one side, I stared, stared at the other – aged what, three? – saw patterns, squiggles, hieroglyphics as meaningful as Sanskrit is to me now, and longed to understand, willed myself to be able to comprehend it. Could not.

Then, click, no time has passed, it seems, and I am reading *Alice in Wonderland* under the bedclothes and *Great Expectations* behind the sofa, and Bunyan and Kingsley and *Five Go to Smuggler's Top*.

But, strangely, I cannot remember a time when I could not write – not simply hold a pen, form letters and words, but write stories, or find it the one and only, the best thing, what I could do

and do well and knew that I did it well, in exactly the same way, I am sure, that an athletic child, fast runner, high jumper, strong swimmer, can do it and loves doing it, exults in it and in knowing how well it can. The joy lies in both the doing and the knowledge.

And here they come again, over my shoulder, whispering in my ear, those questions, insistent. Why? How and why, but the greatest of these is why. I think I know, at least in part, for myself, at any rate.

The answers lie in childhood, of course, like most, and some are obvious, some obscure; they have to do with being an only child, not having too many companions of my own age living nearby, long, cold winters in the north of England, of early and dark and no television and parents reading every evening, piles of library books, novels by the bed and the fireside chairs. And the accidents of inheritance – a vivid imagination, an interest in the worlds behind this world, seeing things in dark places, inventing, supposing. All those and more. The usual reasons. But there is another.

Graham Greene says it for me, as he says many things that are wise and true, in fiction and in essays.

By 1969, I had written a very great deal of totally commonplace juvenilia, sagas in exercise books, a nativity play for my class to act, long, long poems about love and death and my own adolescent feelings, nothing special, except to me – practice work, apprentice stuff. Necessary. Then, in between O levels and A levels and a university degree, two novels, both of them dreadful, necessarily so, yet published, when I was 19 and 21. But they were false starts, I had not found my own voice, what to say, the way to say it. Then, having to earn a living, and without any other career in mind, or aptitude for one, reviewing books, doing odd jobs to pay the rent, waiting, waiting for the moment. I knew it would come, did not know how or when, when the first proper book would come to me, fully formed like Athena out of Zeus's head, and I would be away at last. Meanwhile, I was frustrated, restless, while the work I was to do brewed, marinated in my un- – or is it

sub- ? – conscious. Matured. Oh, I know that now, it is all very well, but at the time I did not and was like a caged bear, going in circles, desperate, endlessly in search of my self. I knew I would be a writer, was a writer, that it was all I was, made endless false starts. How long, O Lord?

It all came together at once. Looking back I see how things formed a pattern and fell carefully into place. I lost my reviewing job on the local paper, I had no money, long, long days and an overdraft – nothing like a bit of starvation to stimulate creative thought. There were no books of other people's to read and pass judgement upon, week in week out, and get in the way of producing my own. The first, real, right and true idea came to me, the gift from heaven, and at the same time I found my own style, my voice, my way of telling it, and it felt as if it had been somewhere very near all along, waiting, just out of reach. I did not work at it, I simply heard the first sentences in my head, as I have heard everything I have ever written since, and recognized them, at once, as what I had been waiting for, and I was away.

The excitement, the sense of rightness, the joy and the satisfaction, are hard to convey now, even hard to remember exactly – but I can, when I try.

The following year, Graham Greene's *Collected Essays* were published. I read them, with interest and admiration, but more important, with repeated cries of recognition and agreement. Here was the articulation of what I had found to be true myself. Greene told what had happened to him at the beginning of his career as a novelist, answered the question why. The book has been one of my two writer's bibles ever since. (The other is Virginia Woolf's *A Writer's Diary*.) I return to them again and again, they are inexhaustible mines of inspiration, I re-read once, twice a year from cover to cover, and then, odd chapters and paragraphs at odd moments, recall and am replenished anew.

The opening chapter of Greene's book *The Lost Childhood* is one of the most fascinating, revelatory, intelligent and beautifully balanced pieces I have ever read on the subject of reading and

childhood, and the formation of the creative imagination. In it, Greene describes with tremendous power the books that first excited and inspired him, when he was a young boy, those that switched on the light for him, books by Rider Haggard, Percy Masterman, Stanley Weyman. He devoured them, he did not merely read and enjoy, they became part of him forever. Two in particular were the keys to his future as a writer: *King Solomon's Mines*, and *The Viper of Milan* by Marjorie Bowen. From the day he took that down from the library shelf, Greene writes, 'the future, for better or worse, really struck. From that moment, I began to write.'

A few paragraphs later, he tries to work out exactly why. 'I think it was Miss Bowen's apparent zest that made me want to write. One could not read her without believing that to write was to live, and to enjoy.'

Yes, yes, that's it, so it was for me (though with other books), so my own imagination was fired. It is not in any way a matter of mere copying, the desire to imitate, it goes far deeper than that. As Graham Greene, the boy, read certain books desperately, feverishly, so I read, and the books, the worlds that the writers had created, places, characters, scenes, these landscapes of the imagination, lived for me and I lived within them, were far more real than reality. Everyday life was a pale, dull, insignificant business by comparison, to be hurried through so that I could return to that far, far better world. The quality of what I read was almost irrelevant, and in the end, simply took care of itself. In any case it is often the books of lesser literary merit that prove the most inspirational in this way. It is not what they are in themselves, so much as what they become to that one reader and future writer, what he makes of them.

I read, then, *Pilgrim's Progress*, *Bleak House* and *Barnaby Rudge*, *Wuthering Heights*, *The Mayor of Casterbridge*, the Bible, *Alice*, John Buchan, Enid Blyton, Conan Doyle, Poe, *Jamaica Inn*. There were many more, thousands probably, which I skimmed over the surface of like a water skier, and remember nothing about; they

made no impression of any lasting kind. Others, like Jane Austen, I realized that I should admire, did so, dutifully, but which left me cold. Later came a very few contemporary writers who lit that light, albeit less brightly. The opening sentence of Greene's essay is, 'Perhaps it is only in childhood that books have any deep influence on our lives ... what do we ever get nowadays from reading to equal the excitement and the revelation of those first fourteen years?'

As I grow older, although I read a few modern novelists, it is to those early books that I return and return, to Dickens, Hardy, Carroll, Buchan, Conan Doyle, Poe, du Maurier, Greene himself, Bunyan, Virginia Woolf. I read them for themselves, but much more importantly, for inspiration, which I always get, and it is new and fresh each time, it never fails. It is so difficult to explain. When I read these writers I am filled with that incomparable excitement that makes me long to take the next step on my own, at once, to do it, to write, like that. Not the same as that, no. But to create for myself, to imagine, to convey, to conjure up worlds, atmospheres, scenes, people, and carry off the reader with the same exhilaration I myself have known.

I have heard writers declare that they are in love with words. I do not understand what they mean. Words are tools, like bricks. I can be in love with a great house, but the materials themselves do not interest. I do not pore over dictionaries, I am uninterested in derivations. But I am made passionate, stirred to admiration and new visions, by great, fictional prose, mighty descriptive passages, that create new worlds, paint great pictures – the opening para-graphs of *Bleak House*, the 'Time Passes' section of Virginia Woolf's *To the Lighthouse*, they hold atmosphere, mystery, truth, and above all, they make me want to do that, too. That is why, finally, for me, why nothing else has ever satisfied and exhilarated me in the same way, or seemed remotely as important – except the births of my three children, which is another matter. Or perhaps it is not.

I have heard them say, oh, I adore writing, just writing, anything

at all. Well, perhaps there was a time, but no, I don't really understand that either. Letters, reviews, introductions, essays, speeches – I loathe doing them, try my best to get out of it all, I would be perfectly happy never again to set pen to paper, save for this, what matters above all, the writing of fiction, the glee when realization dawns that a new one is there, waiting in the wings, waiting for me to turn to it, the intoxication of the planning out, the notebooks, the thinking about it in the bath, in the garden, waking and sleeping, hearing the paragraphs in my head as I write, seeing the scenes to be set, and simultaneously re-reading any of those writers with the old flame of excitement, and sense of power. Me too, me too. And I can, I know I can.

I part company with Greene in the second half of his revelatory sentence about *The Viper of Milan*. One could, he says, not read Miss Bowen without believing that to write was to live, and to enjoy. Yes, oh yes. But then he continues, '. . . and before one had discovered one's mistake, it was too late, – the first book one does enjoy.'

But I have never stopped enjoying, writing fiction has never failed me, though of course there are the dull bits, the bad days. But the more I write, the more clearly I see that even the dull bits, the chores, can be avoided. Greene again, in one of his masterly essays on Henry James, says, 'The moment comes to every writer worth consideration when he faces for the first time something which he knows he cannot do. It is the moment by which he will be judged, the moment when his individual technique will be evolved. For technique is above everything else a means of evading the personally impossible, of disguising deficiency.'

I have sometimes stood in front of a novel to be written, and it has been like a mountain, I have said, 'Oh no, no, this time you have gone too far, I simply cannot, there is no way I can.' Most of all I felt it before a novel I wrote about the First World War, called *Strange Meeting*. But inside, with glee, I knew I was lying, that I could not, yet ultimately, I could pretend that I could, and

so I would, and did. Don't look down. That's the trick. I never do. And as for the dull bits, I realized, with even more glee quite some years ago, that what Greene says about James and technique is true in a very special way. The novelist can do anything, is all powerful. As the child says at age four or five, 'You can't make me do anything I don't want to.' It's as true for the novelist. I simply do not have to do the chores, write the dull bits. I leave them out. Leave the reader to make huge leaps. And the best thing of all is that it works far, far better. It is boring to read a book in which we are made to plod anxiously all the way from A to B. Even more boring to write one. Hop, skip and jump, like Alice over the hedges between the chess squares. Simple.

Heady stuff. Writing is. Gets more so. *That's* why. That's all, really.

Otherwise I would not dream of doing it. Not even for ready money.

ME MAKING MONEY

Lucy Ellmann

As soon as I sat down to begin, all my subject matter retreated before my eyes through sheer terror. The self-discipline involved in starting and continuing and possibly even finishing a book became an issue. I HAVE no self-discipline – if novels really depended on that, I wouldn't have written any. Mine are the result of pure stagnation.

Lucy Ellmann is a critic as well as the author of two novels. Her first novel, *Sweet Desserts*, was awarded the *Guardian* Fiction Prize. She is currently adapting her second novel, *Varying Degrees of Hopelessness*, as a film.

I came from a literary family in which it was very hard to get a word in edgewise. My sister and brother were both older and cleverer. I never won an argument. Both my parents were literary scholars. They had guided my reading all my life. I didn't read a thriller until my mid-twenties. I knew there was only one novelist of real note in the twentieth century: James Joyce. So the act of contributing my own little bit of creative writing to the over-abundance of contemporary fiction did not seem to me a wholly respectable one. The first affront to my family, which they didn't acknowledge at the time, was in climbing that fence, from the sophisticated art of literary criticism, interpretation and exegesis, to producing the actual junk to be criticized. I did it for the money.

I was commissioned to write my first novel, *Sweet Desserts*, one night when I went over to a friend's house for dinner. The friend was Alexandra Pringle, then an editor at Virago Press and now at Hamish Hamilton. I thought it was a joke at first, and laughed. But by the end of the evening, my idea of myself had taken a definite turn for the better – was I, besides being a failed academic, perhaps a novelist? I certainly wanted to be one, though I had not dared write fiction since my early teens, when my macabre, despairing scribbles began to depress me, and I had turned to visual art as being vaguer.

Alexandra not only hit a nerve, though, by reminding me of the art form I understand and cherish above the others, but she offered me the unaccustomed dignity of making a little money. It

was merely £1,000 (£350 on signing the contract, £350 on delivery, £300 on publication), but at the age of twenty-seven or so, I had managed to progress from being a student to being a mother and a student, without yet breaking free of the financial support of my parents, who were generous to a fault. The idea of ME MAKING MONEY fascinated me (still does). And, most tempting of all, she offered her support, which included a great many pleasant drinking sessions and phone calls, an extremely unbusinesslike arrangement which was the only type of arrangement I could have tolerated (and ditto, she still does).

I was never sure if she was just sick of hearing my compulsive ramblings about my life, or entertained by them, but I was pleased to be asked to put them down in writing.

As soon as I sat down to begin, all my subject matter retreated before my eyes through sheer terror. The self-discipline involved in starting and continuing and possibly even finishing a book became an issue. I HAVE no self-discipline – if novels really depended on that, I wouldn't have written any. Mine are the result of pure stagnation. I quickly went into a decline, from which friends tried to rouse me with advice. One said I should just sit down every day and write whatever came into my head. But I knew this would lead to adolescent-style outpourings that I would never be able to reread. The raw stuff in my head is not worth hearing. My father, more helpfully, when I was thinking of giving up, told me that it was at that moment that one is often near a breakthrough – encouragement I cling to every time I am totally stumped. I began to jot down the briefest of notes to myself, ones that I hoped would be bearable (and legible) enough to reread some other day. These pieces of paper later turned up, got read, despised, and rewritten, until a big enough pile had accumulated.

I had thought at first that I would write about my (failed) marriage – having heard that most first novels are autobiographical, I was content that mine would be too. The trouble was, as far as the marriage was concerned, I couldn't remember any of it. I

had not been happy, so had wisely converted the whole experience into a blank. In fact, most of my life was a blank for the same reason. Realizing there wasn't a moment to lose, I managed to get down what I could remember about my husband before it was gone forever. This mainly involved a vision of him doing *The Times* crossword.

But I was startled as soon as I began to write about myself, to find that my behaviour was inexplicable without reference to my sister. I had always emulated her, observed her, copied her. I wasn't sure any of my memories, let alone my opinions, were not actually hers. So it became a book tangentially about *her*, in terms of *me*; how annoying such an indulgence is, coming from a little sister, was not at the time clear to me. I feared her wrath, but felt I was writing out of love and hoped, rather romantically, that that would be the final impression she got. I was not overly vexed by the danger of offending my family with truthfulness, relying, again too romantically, on their reverence for the printed word, as well as their disgust for all those sons, wives and grandchildren of writers who'd made a mess of things for posterity, the prudery of descendants that has so often interfered with scholarship. What I didn't realize was that families are self-censoring bodies; even the most liberal-minded do not wish to be written about. Almost *no one* wants to be written about (compare this fact to the numbers who voluntarily flock to have their portraits painted!). The exception to this rule turned out surprisingly to be a man I said farted a lot in bed. He was glad to be included in the book – showed I cared about him!

When I had amassed enough pieces of paper and the right amount of devil-may-care, I wrote it up over two nights, typing steadily in order to keep the voice the same throughout. By the end I began to feel that everything fitted together, in fact everything new I could think up also seemed to fit. Perhaps I could have gone on writing it forever. But having a practical side which was cautious about over-writing, and a doggy side that likes to be patted, I was eager to show it to Alexandra. The novel worked

for me, but I couldn't be sure it would mean anything to anyone else – the main drawback with autobiographical novels. I was not even sure it *was* a novel!

She reported that she'd laughed and cried, and only wanted me to change a few things. The novel was necessarily a sort of mess, since it was based on life, or my interpretation of life. But she suggested adding a few dates and place names here and there for clarity. She also steered me off the dopey names I'd given to many of my characters, including one named Quagmire. This difficulty with names surfaced too in my second book, but there we allowed it for characters who were meant to be Dickensian stereotypes anyway. I find naming people very embarrassing – it's such a clear confrontation with make-believe, and it's so hard to know if you've got the name right, that I'm tempted to satirize the naming job by using something outrageous. Luckily, Alexandra is ready with the straitjacket.

I also feel very self-conscious inventing plots. They're so silly, they interfere with the serious mood of the confessional; particularly in *Sweet Desserts*, where I wanted to reach some sort of accuracy about life, which depended a good deal on absurd interruptions to the plot, and on natural plotlessness. Plots are fun to read but, for me, very boring to construct, an irritant, an irrelevance. I wanted my characters to stand up to life like penguins in a blizzard, and come through, uneventfully, not wholly intact. What's infinitely mockable, and forever astounding, is that people do carry on through difficult lives that do not reach a satisfying climax. This doesn't make for great theatre, but it's good pathos.

Form and structure have never come easily for me; even in pieces three pages long I have trouble knowing what should come when. I blame it on my bad body-image. At the age of twelve I dressed for Hallowe'en as a Blob, sewing myself into a huge laundry-bag stuffed with fluff. It was a sign of things to come. I see myself as amorphous, amoeboid, with no obvious resemblance to the human form. I quake similarly before amorphous piles of

my bumble-headed ideas. They need a great deal of coaxing and corsetting. They need to be watched sternly, with an eye for ridiculous effulgences, mysterious and inexplicable whimsy, a tendency to *relax*! Fear blobbishness! Never relax.

The success of *Sweet Desserts* was reassuring. I felt that my isolation of the soft spots in myself had touched the required soft spots in other people. The invasion of my own privacy, in writing the book, had been worth it. (And perhaps even the invasion of my family's: the general reception of the book was a comfort when facing my mother's reaction to the fact that I'd killed her off and given my father a second, rather obnoxious, wife, and when facing my sister, who felt betrayed.) But the main effect of the *Guardian* Fiction Prize was that it provoked a letter from a guy I was in love with, who recommended that I gloat on my prize while listening, I think in *bed*, to Glenn Gould. I did listen, as ordered, to Glenn Gould, and gloated on the *letter*, which I considered very promising, which it wasn't, as it turns out. I also got myself an agent, which was a mistake, as it interfered with my relationship with Alexandra. Other than that, success brought a little self-respect, and too much publicity. I do not WANT interviewers to write about me – they're stealing MY MATERIAL!

FLESHING MY CHARACTERS
Deborah Moggach

Once a character has gelled it's an unmistakable sensation, like an engine starting up within one's body. From then onwards one is driven by this other person, seeing things through their eyes, shuffling round the shops as a 57-year-old divorced man and practically feeling one has grown a beard.

Deborah Moggach has written ten novels and many short stories. Two of her novels, *Stolen* and *To Have and to Hold*, started life as TV series and she is adapting her latest novel, *The Stand-In*, for the Hollywood screen.

FLESHING MY CHARACTERS

Creating people is a fascinating business. Some characters start to live and breathe almost without one's help, whereas others – despite huffings and puffings on the author's part – stubbornly refuse to spring to life and remain stillbirths. The funny thing is that I don't think readers can always detect which ones have worked for the author and which haven't; there are so many tricks to cover this up.

What's interesting is that it doesn't depend on the character's age, sex or class. Novelists are hermaphrodites and should be able to slide into other people's skins regardless of gender. In fact, some of my least successful characters have been women of my own age and background; I haven't quite got the hang of them, maybe because they are too close to me, too blurred to get into focus. My test of whether they have worked is to imagine them in various situations – stuck in a lift, say, or riding a horse. Anything, really. And if they have gelled I know exactly how they would behave. From then on I'm able to become them, and act them out for myself.

When I'm creating them, the moment they are realized is triggered in various ways. Take Desmond. He is a middle-aged coach driver in a novel of mine, and he was triggered off, way back in the seventies, by the sight of a coach being loaded up with CND campaigners. The driver stood there, smoking a cigarette, and I imagined what he thought of all those dungaree'd women, 'lentil eaters and lesbians', and how his attitude to them might alter if his own Armageddon loomed up – the discovery that he himself was suffering from an incurable illness. I wrote a short

story about this but he still refused to go away and so, altered but still sort of recognizable, Desmond landed the starring role in a novel of his own.

Sometimes a person gels when I see a face on a bus, or even the TV. Or when I see a house and I realize that it's just the sort of place in which they grew up. When I was driving along the A40 one day I glimpsed a collapsing pig farm; one of those places full of disintegrating lorry containers and old double-decker buses. I saw it so fleetingly, yet at that moment I pictured the narrator of my novel, *Porky*, stepping fastidiously through the mud; I literally *saw* her, although there was nobody there, and by the time I drove into London her whole story had come to me. She had almost told it to me herself.

More recently I was planning a novel about a man who had a lot of ex-wives. He sprang into life once I had pinpointed where he lived: one of those sooty blocks of mansion flats on the Edgware Road. For days I sat in my car, opposite the building, and pictured him shuffling out – big, bearded, wearing espadrilles with the backs squashed down and pulling along one of those matted little dogs that looks as if it has been run over. By this time his name had come to me – Russell Buffery. I knew he would shuffle along to the local pub, because he was a boozer. I knew he would shuffle along to the chemist's, because he was a hypochondriac and needed to buy Algipan for his heart and Fybogel for his bowels, which were always giving him trouble. I followed him to the bottle bank. He was a late but enthusiastic convert to this and glared at people who threw green bottles into the clear container and clear bottles into the green, until he became uncomfortably aware that wine dregs from his own bottles were trickling down his sleeve.

There are other tricks I use, like asking myself questions about the character's past. Were they bullied at school? What was their first car, their first sexual experience? Another way to thicken them up is to construct their obituary and then add other people's views of them; the *Independent* does this when it carries a running

obituary over several days. This way one gets another angle on a person – from an old schoolfriend, say, or someone who was in the Merchant Navy with them. This stops a character from hardening into stereotype because one can see how they alter in the company of different people. My aim (not always achieved) is to make a character solid and recognizable as a type, yet filled with the contradictions and surprises we all have within us.

If I can't picture my character's face I find it useful to pin up a photo of somebody who resembles them. In the case of my man with all the ex-wives I had a photo of Jack Trevor Story sitting in his dressing gown, looking beleaguered and smoking a cigarette. Michael Gambon is another useful face; he is such a chameleon actor that he works for a lot of middle-aged men. If I pin up his picture, or have it in my head, I can talk to him and he answers back in character. *And* I don't have to pay him a fee.

Once a character has gelled it's an unmistakable sensation, like an engine starting up within one's body. From then onwards one is driven by this other person, seeing things through their eyes, shuffling around the shops as a 57-year-old divorced man and practically feeling one has grown a beard. Looking at women, too, the way a man looks at them. It's so strange, swapping sex. I wonder if male novelists get phantom period pains. Novelists are actors – luckier than actors, actually, because we can become our own characters and make up our own lines.

I always start with the outline of a story, but once a character gets going they push it off in their own direction. It's like driving a carriage which is being pulled by particularly sportive horses. I know the destination, but they may decide how to get there. As soon as I know my main characters, they help me create the others. For instance, once Russell Buffery was fixed in my mind I knew that one of his ex-wives would be a neurotic arty type who wore layers of clothes – sort of Miss Havisham meets the Incas – and who went to primal therapy groups. And that an earlier wife would be an ex-actress who ran an antiques stall – one of those women with a sheepskin coat and a smoker's cough, whose

lipstick comes off on their front teeth. My hero collaborated with me on his own past; we discovered it together.

What gets really interesting is when one adapts this into drama – turning one's novel into a TV or film script. One's imaginary characters are going to have to speak, for real; they are literally going to become flesh and blood. Their interior life has to be dismantled and rebuilt as action; their thoughts have to disappear and be recycled as voice-over or dialogue. They themselves have to be given up, like a child for adoption. Their past has to be given to the actor to be incorporated into his or her performance. The same with one's imaginary homes – the places inside one's head have to be discovered by location scouts; the furniture inside one's head has to be constructed by designers. The professionals take over. It's like opening up one's garden to the public.

Often, of course, it's not at all how one imagined it – how could it? It's like picturing an unknown town – Bruges, say – and then going there for the weekend; it is never as one guessed and afterwards it is hard to remember just what one's original picture was. Sometimes the other people who are now involved get it utterly wrong. A scruffy bedsit becomes a chic apartment – TV often cleans things up – or one's heroine, whose children have just been abducted, appears weeping at the police station but sporting a pair of terrifically glamorous earrings. Who would put on a pair of earrings when their children have been stolen?

Actors take over one's characters and change them for ever. Each actor brings his or her own history to the part, and often quarrels with one's lines. Discussing this can thicken up a character in one's head; sometimes, embarrassingly, it can reveal just how thin a character was to begin with. One has to keep this secret from everyone – especially the actors. An author must never, ever say, 'Gosh, I don't know.'

If a novel is a noun, drama is a verb. Everything has to be put into action. Looking at a scene, you don't ask 'What does it show?' but 'What happens?' The story has to be dismantled and reassembled – dismembering one's own baby – and the biggest

temptation is to be retentive and cling on to the bits one likes. Screenplay writers have to shed their egocentricity; things are going to be changed, they are part of a team, their script is just a blueprint. I try not to look at a novel of mine when I'm adapting it; I try to start from scratch.

What helps is some big jolt that throws the whole mechanism awry. For instance, I've just adapted my coach driver novel. In it, a man – Desmond – travels all over England looking for his lost son, a boy he has never seen. Though the novel is good for drama in that it's highly visual – a huge coach ploughing through city centres, a sort of Magical Mystery Tour – during it he is mostly alone. That's hopeless for drama; there are only so many shots you can show of a man's face. So the producer suggested bringing in another character right at the beginning, joining Desmond in his coach and building up a relationship with him. This broke the backbone of my original book and I had to reassemble it very differently. This in turn liberated the rest of the story. When it is actually filmed more changes will be made. Who knows? Maybe we'll get Michael Gambon to play the starring role and the whole thing will come full circle.

The other novel of mine that I've adapted – *The Stand-In* – is about a movie star and her stand-in. This, too, had to be reconstructed because the producers wanted a different person to be murdered at the end. It gave the story a better dramatic thrust. In this case I knew the probable cast, so I pinned up their photos and put my words into their mouths to see if it worked. As it's set in the movie business I also pinned up photos of film shoots. While I mouthed my dialogue into the mirror – looking quite demented – I played soundtracks of Hollywood thrillers which got me into a movie mood. I also read stacks of screenplays – proper typescripts, badly photocopied, full of 'angle on' and 'dissolve to' – which made the whole thing feel much more real and possible than reading books of screenplays published by Faber.

That's one way round. But I've also done the whole thing reversed – that is, writing TV scripts which I've then turned into

novels. This is almost more fascinating. Writing a script means you see characters in terms of what they do and what they say. It's a public business. You write a scene that mentions casually that the hero collects Dinky cars and – lo and behold – someone from props ransacks London to find miniature Ford Populars to put on the mantelpiece. These dressed sets are yours and yet not yours – already they are being filtered through someone else's imagination. When we write a novel we create our own interiors; when we write a script we are giving orders.

The same thing with locations. With my TV serial *Stolen*, my words sent a crew and cast to the other side of the world, to film in Karachi. What power! All those hotel bookings, gippy tummies and street scenes full of scores of extras and hundreds of onlookers. The floor manager even had to learn 'Quiet please! Roll to record!' in Urdu. Back in Ashford High Street they put up Christmas-tree lights in April, prompting a passing shopper, who didn't realize what was happening, to turn to her friend and say 'Goodness, it gets earlier each year, doesn't it?'

When it comes to the characters the whole process becomes more complicated – much more complicated than when one is simply writing a novel. Each character consists of several different versions who have to finally merge together in your eventual novel, like a hologram. First, when you are writing the script, there are the people you dreamed up in your head. Then along come the real human beings, with their own opinions and their surprisingly different faces from those you have imagined. In turn, they have to get dressed in their costumes and make their own transitions. For the period of filming they embark on their own journey, your script simply a chart in their hands. You watch with fascinated anxiety. If they are good they flesh out your people and add their own bits of business. By now you have forgotten what your original characters were like; they have faded away.

Then filming ends and the final stage begins: turning it into a novel. The actors leave, but their creations remain. These you shepherd back into your head, like a farmer bringing in his flock

for the winter. Now comes the slow, interior process of turning it back into fiction. Suddenly you are wonderfully free – you are director, editor, props, an entire crew rolled into one. Released from the budget, you can create scenes in Timbuktu if you want to. Liberated from the banned flashback (too slow for drama) you recreate interior monologues and past lives. You give your characters childhoods, parents, and all the things TV cannot contain in its little box. You bring in memories and metaphors, possible only on the printed page. Eagerly you rummage in your wastepaper basket and unscrumple the bits of script you had to throw away. Often these are your favourites – the funniest or most quirky bits that had to be cut because they didn't push along the action. Or maybe they are the bits that couldn't be used because it meant night shooting on triple-time union rates. Who cares now? Your own budget is limitless.

I wonder, in the end, how much it shows. Clues to a novelization are lots of dialogue (lifted straight from the script) and a plot with an exterior rather than an interior pace. This will probably include a regularly spaced number of cliffhangers, vestigial relics of the original commercial breaks and ends of episodes. Depending on how good the novel is, or how hastily written, these may be more or less obvious. With any luck they may only be glimpsed by experts, like ancient tumuli spotted from the air by a qualified archaeologist.

The one thing your readers will never guess is your large, invisible cast of collaborators: the actors and crew. They themselves don't know how they guide your fingers over the typewriter keys. They are your ghost writers. And if the novel isn't much good, you can always blame *them*.

One last image – one of those real jolts. I was in my car, stuck in a traffic jam in Camden High Street. I was in a hurry; I had to collect my children from school and I was late. I sat there, fuming and fretting. And then I noticed that the vehicles blocking the way were a whole fleet of London Weekend TV lorries, parked in the road and holding up the traffic. It was only then that I realized

they were filming *my own drama* – the TV series that I had written. My words had brought the traffic to a standstill from Camden Town all the way to the Euston Road. What an achievement! One novelist had managed to gridlock half of North London. Now *that's* power.

HEARING THEM SPEAK

Penelope Fitzgerald

When the dialogue begins, the tempo slows down to the pace of the story itself. The reader understands very well that he is being drawn close in. He, too, is relieved to hear what the voices are like.

Penelope Fitzgerald has three times been short-listed for the Booker Prize and was a winner with her 1979 novel, *Offshore*. Her most recent novel, *Gate of Angels*, was also short-listed for the *Irish Times*/Aer Lingus Prize.

Of course you want to hear their voices. Having summoned up these human beings, you want to know what they sound like. In the novels I used to read, and still do for that matter, people spoke 'sharply', 'reluctantly', 'with unaffected warmth', 'with a touch of bitterness'. They spoke of 'taking her hand in his', or 'whipping out a gun'. These last two, of course, are actions, and must be described if anything is going to be understood at all, but when I'm writing myself I have a slight sense of failure every time I put in a 'sharply' or a 'reluctantly'. The characters and the situation between them ought to have made it clear already how sharp, or how reluctant they are.

When the dialogue begins, the tempo slows down to the pace of the story itself. The reader understands very well that he is being drawn close in. He, too, is relieved to hear what the voices are like.

What is the first thing he is going to hear? The first novel I did was called *The Bookshop*. In the opening paragraph Florence Green, who is worried about whether she should open a bookshop in a small town on the East Coast, dreams of a heron she once saw

flying across the estuary and trying, while it was on the wing, to swallow an eel which it had caught. The eel, in turn, was struggling to escape from the gullet of the heron and appeared a quarter, a half, or occasionally three-quarters of the way out. The indecision expressed by both creatures was pitiable. They had taken on too much.

I now think this was a mistake, because dreams in fiction are just

as tedious as people's dreams in real life. I should have done better to start straight away with Florence Green courageously asking the bank manager for a loan, so that the first speaking voice would be the manager's, suggesting in itself the strength of the sluggish opposition ranged against her.

At the beginning of *Gate of Angels* Fred Fairly, a lecturer in physics, is biking into Cambridge on a stormy day. Acquaintances catch up with him one by one.

He was shouting. It was like sea-bathing . . . A whole group went by, then one of them detached himself and was riding alongside.

'Skippey!'

He couldn't hear what Skippey said, so dropped back and came up on the other side, the lee side.

'You were saying?'

'Thought is blood,' Skippey replied.

Fred speaks for the first time in public, so that there is likely to be a difference between what he is saying and what he would like to say. In this way I hoped to get the words to work twice for me.

You can, of course, write a novel entirely in dialogue. One writer who did this was a late-nineteenth-century woman of the world called (or calling herself) 'Gyp'. Henry James admired her, and thought of doing the same thing in *The Awkward Age*, but fortunately didn't. And you can manage without dialogue, as Swift did in *Gulliver's Travels*, where all the conversations are reported (except, I think, the Lilliputian words '*Hekina degul*' and '*Borach mivola*'). This is all the more remarkable because *Gulliver*, as a traveller's tale, is necessarily a monologue, and in a monologue above all you feel the need of another voice breaking in, a very different one if possible – like, for instance, Mr Antolini, the corrupt schoolmaster in *Catcher in the Rye*.

But exactly when ought speech to be reported, and when ought it to be out loud? One of the few advantages the novelist has over the dramatist (and they are getting fewer all the time) is that his

passages of dialogue last for a limited time only. The story-teller's instinct, or perhaps his judgement, tells him when they have gone on long enough to make their greatest impact, and when to let the voices fall silent. Kafka's *The Trial* (translated by Willa and Edwin Muir, Gollancz, 1935) opens with the famous incident of K.'s arrest at his lodgings.

'I'd better get Frau Grubach –' said K., as if wrenching himself away from the two men (though they were standing at quite a distance from him) and making as if to go out. 'No,' said the man at the window, flinging a book down on the table and getting up. 'You can't go out, you are arrested.' 'So it seems,' said K. 'But what for?' he added. 'We are not authorised to tell you that. Go to your rooms and wait there. Proceedings have been instituted against you, and you will be informed of everything in due course.' ... 'You'll soon discover that we're telling the truth,' said Franz, advancing on him simultaneously with the other man. They both examined his nightshirt and said he would have to wear a less fancy shirt now, but that they would take charge of this one and the rest of his underwear and, if his case turned out well, restore them later.

The change to reported speech distances you from K.'s visitors, and makes any hope of understanding them, or of the case 'turning out well', seem less and less likely.

While the talking is going on, the novelist has a welcome feeling of relaxation and freedom. There are so many possible variations in dialogue, the most musical of all the novelist's techniques. Confrontation is, of course, only one of them. TV probably conditions us too much to disagreement and insults, the staple of the comedy script. A novelist can allow time, if he wants to, for conversations which just tick over, the dialogue of contentment. Nothing is more extraordinary in *War and Peace* than the last chapters, where the happy (but not perfect) marriages are, as John Bayley has said, 'the equivalent of the Russian victory over Napoleon'. At the Bolkonskys' country home, when Pierre comes back from the wars, the children are in ecstasy because the governess has finished a pair of stockings, and, by a secret known

only to herself, has knitted both of them at once. 'Two of them, two of them,' the children shout. Tolstoy doesn't suggest that this happiness can last. The French invasion lies behind these people, the December revolution is just ahead, but through the children's voices he shows what the nature of happiness is.

Kazuo Ishiguro, the most restrained of contemporary novelists, uses a high proportion of dialogue. His narrators, although apparently as clear as daylight, are ambiguous because they are always self-deceiving. In *A Pale View of Hills* the narrator, Etsuko, is a Japanese woman living in England. She has to come to terms with the present (her daughter has committed suicide) but also with her past. She recalls the 1950s, when she was living in the muddy wasteland outside Nagasaki, and the people who mattered to her then – her irritable husband, her bewildered father-in-law, her friend Mrs Fujiwara who had lost everything and was reduced to keeping a noodle shop, her strange new acquaintance Sachiko who declared or pretended that her American lover was going to pay for her passage back to the States. These are all unsensational people who talk in a quite unsensational way, but with a certain formality and repetitiveness which is understood as Japanese convention.

'In any case, Etsuko, why would he have gone to all this trouble if he wasn't absolutely sincere? Why would he have gone to all this trouble on my behalf? Sometimes, Etsuko, you seem so doubting. You should be happy for me.'

'Yes, of course, I'm very happy for you.'

'But really, Etsuko, it would be unfair to start doubting him after he's gone to all this trouble. It would be quite unfair.'

Gradually these repetitions begin to sound like a ritual whose meaning we are afraid to understand. None of the speakers ever raises their voices. Ishiguro has the chance, at any point, to change the whole tone of his book and to introduce shock or violence, but he never does. Behind everything, however, that is said or done there are recurrent images of hanging and drowning,

rope and water. The sinister enigma of Etsuko's daily life is never quite solved. Nor is the nightmare of Japanese history.

Ishiguro excels at one-to-one dialogue, and it has to be admitted that this is the easiest kind to write. I used to find that after I had got quite a long way with a book I hadn't managed a single scene where more than two people were talking to each other. I still have this difficulty.

In D.H. Lawrence's *Sons and Lovers* William, the collier's eldest son, who has been working in London as a clerk, brings his smart fiancée back to meet the family at Christmas.

She glanced round the kitchen. It was small and curious to her, with its glittering kissing-bunch, its evergreens behind the pictures, its wooden chairs and little deal table. At that moment Morel came in.

'Hello, dad!'

'Hello, my son! Tha's let on me!'

The two shook hands, and William presented the lady. She gave the same smile that showed her teeth.

'How do you do, Mr Morel?'

Morel bowed obsequiously.

'I'm very well, and I hope so are you. You must make yourself very welcome.'

'Oh, thank you,' she said, rather amused.

'You will like to go upstairs,' said Mrs Morel.

'If you don't mind; but not if it is any trouble to you.'

'It is no trouble. Annie will take you. Walter, carry up this box.'

'And don't be an hour dressing yourself up,' said William to his betrothed.

Annie took a brass candlestick, and, too shy almost to speak, preceded the young lady to the front bedroom, which Mr and Mrs Morel had vacated for her. It, too, was small and cold by candlelight. The colliers' wives only lit fires in bedrooms in case of extreme illness.

'Shall I unstrap the box?' asked Annie.

'Oh, thank you very much!'

It isn't only the cross-currents of feeling here that Lawrence does

so well, but the integration of five voices and five distinct points of view to make the whole complex family-kitchen situation. He worked hard on his dialogue, as his manuscript corrections show, and yet it was so much a natural element to him that he could risk all kinds of bizarre effects. In *Kangaroo* the speakers can hardly hear each other over the roar of the sea, and in *The Captain's Doll* the lovers' voices are carried away by the noise of the car, so that the Captain has to shout in Hannele's ear: 'When my wife died I knew I couldn't love any more.' *Women in Love*, which begins with dialogue, also ends with it. Ursula tells Birkin that it's out of the question for him to have 'eternal union' with one man, as well as one woman:

'You can't have it because it's false, impossible,' she said.
'I don't believe that,' he answered.

Lawrence is also, when he wants to be, a faultless impersonator. He can 'do' voices, tones, accents and dialects, although this is something a lot of writers are good at; it may have been why they started to write in the first place. Joyce, I suppose, took impersonation about as far as it can go, imitating even the cabhorse. Novelists, however, quite often prefer to heighten the dialogue and, in general, to make the speakers more acute and knowing and more articulate than they are likely to be in real life. Henry James did this, Ivy Compton Burnett did, so did Samuel Beckett in his novels:

What a joy it is to laugh from time to time, [Father Ambrose] said. Is it not? I said. It is peculiar to man, he said. So I have noticed, I said . . . Animals never laugh, he said. It takes us to find that funny, I said. What? he said. It takes us to find that funny, I said loudly. He mused. Christ never laughed either, he said, as far as we know. He looked at me. Can you wonder? I said.

This kind of dialogue shows us what we *could* say if we had our wits about us, and gives us its own peculiar satisfaction.

I ought perhaps to try to say something about the great high

points, but I should like to end instead with one of dialogue's special effects which, as far as I know, has never had a name given to it.

Before they separated, however ... Mr Bob Sawyer, thrusting his fore-finger between two of Mr Pickwick's ribs, and thereby displaying his native drollery, and his knowledge of the anatomy of the human frame, at one and the same time, inquired, 'I say, old boy, where do you hang out?'

Mr Pickwick replied that he was at present suspended at the George and Vulture.

If Dickens had made Pickwick say 'I am at present suspended &c &c' the effect would be gone, vanished into the vast limbo of failed ironies.

In Jane Austen's *Persuasion*, kindly Mrs Musgrove has to think what to say to Mrs Croft, who is an Admiral's wife.

'What a great traveller you must have been, ma'am!' said Mrs Musgrove to Mrs Croft.

'Pretty well, ma'm, in the fifteen years of my marriage, although many women have done more. I have crossed the Atlantic four times, and have been once to the East Indies, and back again; and only once, besides being in different places about home – Cork, and Lisbon, and Gibraltar. But I never went beyond the Straits – and never was in the West Indies. We do not call Bermuda or Bahamas, you know, the West Indies.'

Mrs Musgrove had not a word to say in dissent; she could not accuse herself of ever having called them anything in the whole course of her life.

Does Mrs Musgrove in fact say anything at all? Again, in Christine Brooke-Rose's *Amalgamemnon*, the speaker is Cassandra, a teacher of classical languages who has been made redundant by the cuts. She is also doomed, like her Greek prototype, to foretell the future, but in vain.

Tomorrow he'll say Sandra my love when shall I see you again I'll be free

tomorrow, I'll be free Friday Saturday Sunday. Friday Saturday Sunday I must prepare my classes correct papers no I must weed the vegetable garden clean the pigsties wash my hair meet Orion invent Andromeda from time to time unheeded and unhinged discover the grammar of the universe.

What has been said so far? Nothing. 'If he were someone in a nineteenth-century novel I might ironically detach him,' Cassandra thinks, but *Amalgamemnon* is a post-modernist novel and Christine Brooke-Rose uses 'non-realized tenses' to conjure up spoken voices. However, like Dickens and Jane Austen, she can remind us that one of the privileges of dialogue is silence.

THICKENING MY PLOTS

Patricia Highsmith

When I am thickening my plots, I like to think 'What if . . .
What *if* . . .' Thus my imagination can move from the likely,
which everyone can think of, to the unlikely-but-possible,
my preferred plot.

Patricia Highsmith is renowned for her literary thrillers. Her first novel, *Strangers on a Train*, was filmed by Alfred Hitchcock and her fourth, *The Talented Mr Ripley*, was awarded the Edgar Allen Poe Scroll by the Mystery Writers' Guild of America. Her most recent novel is *Ripley Under Water*.

THICKENING MY PLOTS

When writers are invited to tell how they write a short story or a novel, they are also cautioned not to write a 'how to' piece. And yet what else can it be, if a writer tries to state in declarative sentences how he gets from idea to something on paper?

I think of a short story as a brief work, an anecdote almost, and what makes an anecdote interesting? Something amusing or engaging from the start. It is the same with a joke, except that the very word 'joke' captures an audience, if one promises to tell one. In a short story, the gripping element need not be funny, but perhaps unusual, even unfortunate. I speak now of the origin of a story in the writer's mind or imagination.

For example, I had to see if I had locked a door one night – I think in a rented house somewhere – and found that I hadn't. An idea came to me as I was locking the door: suppose I was locking an intruder in with me? After all, I had just heard an odd noise. I probably did not make a note that night, just fell asleep thinking about the possibilities.

A few days later, I had thought of something more complicated: a wife is alone for a weekend in a new house, as her husband has to be away on business. Hearing a noise, she goes downstairs and locks the kitchen door, only to realize a minute later that someone is in the living-room with a torch, collecting anything of value such as silver. The robber in stocking mask is quite sure of himself, and tells the woman to keep quiet and she won't get hurt. He takes a sackful of loot out to his companion who is waiting in a car some yards away in the drive. My story becomes 'a story' when the woman decides to defend herself: she picks up a metal

stool in the kitchen, and hits the man in the forehead when he re-enters the kitchen, again alone. The 'victim' has suddenly become 'the murderer'. The second man departs in the car, alarmed by getting no response from his partner when he shouts to him. The woman reports the incident. There is a corpse on the kitchen floor – but under the circumstances, the woman is not going to be accused of murder, or accused of anything. She even gets a word of praise from police and neighbours.

The problem is that the deed troubles the woman. She must narrate the story over and over, when she goes out to dinner parties or has coffee with a friend. Each narration is like a confession. It – her compulsion to confess – bothers her husband, but he can't talk his wife out of it. The story is called 'Something You Have to Live With'. When I was writing it and had reached the part where the woman uses the kitchen stool as a weapon, I may have thought that in an emotional sense I was 'finished'. That is, I had given myself (and readers too) the satisfaction of believing that unarmed householders *could* hit back at invading thugs. Fine, but not interesting enough. The element of a bad conscience entered, simply because the woman was 'normal', with average reactions to violent deeds. This provided the contrast, therefore the *raison d'être* of the story.

A far more complex 'contrast situation' is described in my novel *The Blunderer*. An 'innocent' man, Walter, married to a shrewish wife, happens to notice a small item in a New York newspaper about a woman found stabbed and throttled to death at the edge of a road near a bus rest-stop, and thinks: could her husband (the item says she was married) have done it? He has zero reason for thinking this, except for the fact the body was a hundred yards or more from the lighted roadside café which was the bus stop. Would a fortyish woman have walked such a distance in the dark with someone she didn't know? Walter is on the right track, but he does not know it. He is at that moment even a bit ahead of the police. If he had only left well enough alone! But his curiosity leads him to look up the husband, who

runs a bookshop. Trouble brews. When I am thickening my plots, I like to think 'What if . . . What *if* . . .' Thus my imagination can move from the likely, which everyone can think of, to the unlikely-but-possible, my preferred plot.

But of course a short story or a novel holds the reader not always by plot, but by atmosphere. Marcel Proust may be the best example, his leisurely and elegant prose leading the reader into the atmosphere of a room, of a village, a garden arbour in that village. Characters are gently introduced one by one, like invited guests arriving for an important occasion. Nothing happens for thirty pages and more, but an enchanted reader keeps on.

When an idea for 'a story' comes, I know almost at once whether it is to be a novel or a short story. For me, the difference hangs on time span: a novel (as I see nearly 300 pages to be written by me) needs a time span of four months, a year, maybe more. In contrast, a short story may be about someone contemplating suicide and a) going through with it, or b) deciding against it, all in ten or twelve pages. But this is idiosyncratic, and de Maupassant and Chekhov have written stories which may span an individual's long life, and describe that life. A novel demands more time to plan than does a short story, and for obvious reasons: there are probably more characters in a novel, and their personalities (and reasons therefore) have to be thought out; often research is necessary in regard to a city, a neighbourhood; notes are scribbled down that may have to be sorted and typed up later.

The important thing is to be sure of oneself before beginning, then even if the writing is slow at first, the writer feels on sure ground – therefore encouraged. The old advice, write about what you know, is still valid, and if what you know about is unusual, like Alaskan homesteading, or action with the Royal Life-boat service in the North Sea, for instance, so much the better. But first, readers want to read about *people*, individuals whom they can believe in, and preferably like a little. A naive, maybe careless but lucky hero or heroine would appeal to readers, I think, because we all worry about not doing the wise thing in a crisis;

and if such a personage comes out alive and successful, the reader gets a lift from it. A reader has to identify – even slightly – with a character or two, otherwise he or she is not going to go on reading. This accounts for the fact that few men read 'women's novels' if the feminine side of things is laid on with a trowel. A man might be curious enough to read a few pages (after all, he may be learning something), but it's a rare thing if a man peruses all three hundred-odd pages of such a book, for the simple reason that he probably can't identify with the heroine. Great novelists like Jane Austen and Leo Tolstoy write with such scope and insight into the personalities of both sexes, that the male or female elements (as such) are forgotten, non-existent compared to the society and story being set forth.

As I write this short article, I wonder how old or young the readers of it will be? In a way, it doesn't matter, not as to my advice here. Some born writers know all that I say here at the age of twelve. The curious thing is that writing becomes a philosophy gradually, or a way of life. Not that one thinks, every day, 'I am a writer.' No, one doesn't have to think it. Being a writer, of fiction, implies a certain turn of mind, a way of seeing things (everything) which is individual to the writer. Nothing to worry about in regard to losing it, as a writer can no more lose it than he can lose his fingerprints.

This reminds me of an important aspect of writing, which might be called style, but I prefer to call it personality (of the writer, of course). But maybe this is because I never thought of acquiring a style. This to me suggests trying to change my hand-writing, which would be nearly impossible and also a meaningless task. However, personality is what we love, or buy, in artists like van Gogh and Toulouse-Lautrec. Instantly recognizable their work is, from as far across a room as one can see. It is the same with writing. We all have our favourites, and love to say, to ourselves usually, 'That's typically Dickens (or maybe Tom Sharpe) and isn't it wonderful!'

In a word, be yourself.

COOKING THE BOOKS

Margaret Forster

I came across a letter of Thackeray's in which he talked of a novel 'a-boilin' up in my interior' . . . But now, fifteen years later, I know they don't always boil up: sometimes the purpose can come before the inspiration.

Margaret Forster, novelist and biographer, was awarded the Royal Society of Literature Award for her biography of Elizabeth Barrett Browning. Her novel, *Have the Men Had Enough?* was short-listed for the *Sunday Express* Award in 1989. She is now working on the authorized biography of Dame Daphne du Maurier.

COOKING THE BOOKS

What an odd thing it is that novelists are always being asked *how* they write their novels and yet hardly ever 'why', a much more interesting question, though miles harder to answer. The facile reply, 'For money', is hardly worth bothering with – of course we all want to earn a living if we can, but that is rarely the mainspring of novels. And yet it seems to me there has to be a reason, even a justification, and that we novelists have to know whether we think we are entertaining or instructing or communicating or even just amusing ourselves – we can't simply shrug and say, 'Don't know.'

I, anyway, feel this, the more novels I have written. When I started off in 1964, I think I was just playing, experimenting, seeing if I could do it, but even then I knew that the desire to try at all arose naturally and was not created in any artificial way by me. I didn't think, 'I want to write a novel', but 'I think there is a novel I want to write'. The feeling would come over me, as I was reading – a slow, excited feeling of 'I can do this, I *want* to do this'. It was a little like a feeling of envy but not exactly envy, more one of recognition that here was a process I loved – being taken into someone else's imagination – and that I too wanted to pull people into mine. I'd become physically restless the better the novel I was reading, longing to try my hand, so eventually I did, not bothering too much about why I wanted to, because I felt such an impetus. Years later I came across a letter of Thackeray's in which he talked of a novel 'a-boilin' up in my interior' and so I thought that was it: the 'why' is answered by saying, 'It boils up in the interior.'

But now, fifteen years later, I know they don't always boil up: sometimes the purpose can come before the inspiration. This has happened to me three times recently and I'm beginning to wonder if there is some deeply significant change going on. The first time was with *Have The Men Had Enough?* This didn't boil up in my interior or anywhere else: it was deliberately manufactured to achieve the little I thought I could achieve. I was determined to *use* the novel to arouse debate – very grand-sounding, but I was feeling furious. For five years I had helped to look after my mother-in-law who suffered from Alzheimer's disease. In 1987 she died after six appalling last months in the geriatric ward of a mental hospital. The experience was terrible and I'd found myself raging at the stupidity and horror of how she died. I'd sat by her bed, watching her die by infinitely slow degrees, until for the last weeks she could not speak, could not see, could not eat, could not move, and all in the most grim, wretched surroundings.

I despised myself for not *doing* anything, for not storming, yelling at whoever ran those hideous wards until either my mother-in-law was put out of her misery or else a way was found for her to continue to live which was not cruel. So I thought I would write a novel after she died, that I would try to use the novel as a vehicle to express my rage and explore the whole dilemma.

Coldly, cunningly, in the six weeks following her death, I wrote *Have The Men Had Enough?* I knew I had to make it as light as possible, since the subject matter was so heavy, and as objective because it was so emotional. I felt I was using every trick in what has been my trade for twenty-five years – like a bricklayer who knows exactly how to lay the foundations so they can bear the load and how to build the wall to take the roof. The novel was all structure – tight, controlled, restrained and the finished thing was a product, an artefact. All the material was at hand, it just needed to be shaped, and it felt very strange to write. I wasn't sitting imagining things but merely calling up from my memory what it had absorbed and inventing only slightly different characters and

lives to fit them. It felt quite satisfactory at the end, though not a novel as I'd thought of novels until then.

Straight afterwards, I wrote a quite different book, a biography, and then found I was once more landing myself with another story which had not just boiled up. This was an historical novel called *Lady's Maid*. Writing the biography of Elizabeth Barrett Browning, I'd become as fascinated by her maid, Elizabeth Wilson, as I was by her, but unfortunately there was very little material on her and no prime source papers at all. Wilson, as she was known, always had to be seen through her mistress's eyes and when I finished the book I was certain that this view had been heavily prejudiced and I thought how I'd like to tell the story the other way round, through Wilson's eyes. But obviously it would have to be a novel, since a biography was impossible with no source material, and I wondered if this would lead me into that grey area called 'faction' which I didn't like the idea of at all. In a way, I suppose it did, because what happened was that through knowing so much about the background to Wilson's life and all the details about the Brownings, I couldn't *not* use it. Instead of the fictional form making me feel free to invent, I found having done E.B.B's biography constrained me – I simply couldn't bring myself to invent things I definitely knew had not happened. All the time I was writing it I was listening carefully to the echoes from the biography and if they didn't sound right I'd stop and re-think. It took a year to complete and even then I'd only got up to Wilson in middle age, and I ended up thoroughly confused about what I'd turned out. This was the novel as substitute biography and I'll never do another.

The third novel which I created, rather than having it arise naturally, was *The Battle for Christabel*. If *Have The Men Had Enough?* was using the novel as a piece of polemic, *The Battle for Christabel* was propaganda. It so happened that several friends in the area of North London where I live had over the previous five years decided to have children without wanting the men to do more than impregnate them. It was all quite deliberate: they were

each between thirty-two and thirty-eight years of age, had always wanted a child. No man, in each case, had come their way in whom they had any real interest and so they decided to go ahead and have a child without any ideas about involving whoever they chose to be the father. Each actually went about getting pregnant in a slightly different way – I mean, one asked an old friend to oblige, who she knew would not want any ties; one slept with three different men without them, or her, knowing who would make her pregnant; one did it through artificial insemination. When they each told me, over a period of time, I seemed appalled. But then, once the various babies were born, I began to think maybe I'd been too hasty with my value judgements and began to ask myself if children really *do* need a father, and also whether an overwhelming urge to have a child on the part of a woman who thinks it all through carefully and is organized and sensible and capable might not be perfectly acceptable. But then one of these friends died and her child was automatically taken into care and I saw a whole new set of problems. So *The Battle for Christabel* became a way of exploring the ethics of women cutting men out of their plans for having children and of what seemed to be a new inclination to use men as studs just as women were for centuries used as breeding machines.

I enjoyed writing it but again I didn't feel this was really a novel. There was a detachment about writing all those three books – polemic, substitute biography and propaganda – which didn't feel right. Nothing boiled up in the interior – it was all boiled up already, all the ingredients and cooking pots to hand, only needing to be mixed, assembled and cooked. Maybe readers can't see the difference but writers always can. Funnily enough, though I'm still obsessed with writing the authorized biography of Daphne du Maurier, now three years on the go, I've lately begun to feel maybe something is genuinely boiling up once more . . . Don't know what exactly, but there is a shadowy vision and odd lines in my head and I know one day it will all look clearer and I'll just have to start, with no notes or plans or any idea where it is going but knowing something is there.

Now that really is a novel.

LITERARY LANDSCAPES

Elizabeth Jolley

It is often for the passages where the writer dwells with loyalty in his landscape that we read certain authors. Often, too, the landscape parallels some of the characters' hidden aspects, which need to be shown rather than told in straight, flat passages of explanatory narrative.

Elizabeth Jolley is an English novelist and short-story writer living in Australia. Her works include *Foxybaby*, *The Newspaper of Claremont Street* and *Woman in a Lampshade*. Her most recent novel is *The Sugar Mother*.

LITERARY LANDSCAPES

Who can be wise, amazed, temperate and furious,
Loyal and neutral, in a moment? No man . . .

I have always expected loyalty from a teapot, and so it is doubly distressing that my indestructible teapot has a small hole in it. Such hypocrisy goes against all ideas of true loyalty. Is it possible to compare human qualities with those of a teapot? Probably not.

The great loyalty of the fiction writer towards the reader is in the attempt to distil from landscape and experience particles of culture and background and to put this material into an available and acceptable form. To be loyal both to background and to reader, the writer needs to exercise judgement in order to select and choose, to concentrate and to refine and to reject non-essentials, so that the best material is offered in the best possible way.

One of the positive aspects of migration is that it demands loyalty of all kinds in all kinds of directions, to the past, to the present and to the self. I came to Western Australia from Britain in the middle of my life. I realize that the freshness of my observation can distort as well as illuminate. The impact of the new country does not obliterate the previous one but sharpens memory, thought and feeling by providing a contrasting theme or setting.

My fiction is not autobiographical but like all fiction it springs from moments of truth and awareness, from observation and experience. The writer tries to develop the moment of truth with the magic of the imagination. The writer usually is loyal to this moment of truth and to the landscape either of his own region or of the region in which the novel or the story is set. I have always felt that the best fiction is regional. It used to be the fashion, or perhaps there was a need, for Western Australian writers to deny

their region. In Europe and in Britain this has never been the case. Writers shamelessly set their work in the places where they live and work. Some years ago an editor told me that I was *revealing* the Western Australian background in a novel by putting in jarrah trees and mentioning that looking westward it was possible to see the sea. The editor's geography was not foolproof, for there are other places in Australia from which the sea can be seen westward. I kept the offending details in the novel.

In *The Return of the Native*, Thomas Hardy created a heath that people still search for. The heath of his imagination is real in that it resembles in all natural ways the heathlands in his part of England. In the places where Hardy *dwells* in the novel there are exquisite passages:

Along the ridge ran a faint foot-track, which the lady followed. Those who knew it well called it a path; and, while a mere visitor would have passed it unnoticed even by day, the regular haunters of the heath were at no loss for it at midnight. The whole secret of following these incipient paths, when there was not light enough in the atmosphere to show a turnpike-road, lay in the development of the sense of touch in the feet, which comes with years of night-rambling in little-trodden spots. To a walker practised in such places a difference between impact on maiden herbage, and on the crippled stalks of a slight footway, is perceptible through the thickest boot or shoe.

If you read Hardy's novels just for the story you might as well hang yourself. It is often for the passages where the writer dwells with loyalty in his landscape that we read certain authors. This landscape is a setting for the characters and events but it is often more than that. In the time of *dwelling*, looking around at the 'little-trodden spots', the writer can suspend action, add to the portrayal of characters and heighten the drama. Often, too, the landscape parallels some of the characters' hidden aspects, which need to be shown rather than told in straight, flat passages of explanatory narrative.

'A Hedge of Rosemary' is the first story I wrote after arriving in

Western Australia. In it there are two contrasting landscapes, an attempt perhaps to close the enormous space between my two worlds. (The journey by ship took just over three weeks.)

When he [the old man] went out in the evening he walked straight down the middle of the road, down towards the river. The evening was oriental, with dark verandahs and curving ornamental roof tops, palm fronds and the long weeping hair of peppermint trailing, a mysterious profile . . . the moon, thinly crescent and frail, hung in the gum leaf lace . . . the magpies caressed him with their cascade of watery music . . .

On my first evening in Western Australia I went out to post a letter, a short way along the road and round a corner. I walked down the middle of the road; the evening was oriental with dark verandahs and curving ornamental rooftops. Back home again, I wrote a few lines of description and followed these immediately with a few words about the stillness and the eerie quietness. And then I wrote of my own longing for the chiming of city clocks through the comforting roar of the city and the friendly screech of trams. I described the heave and roar of the blast furnace and the nightly glow across the sky when the furnace was opened. Recalling the home where I had lived as a child in the Black Country (the industrial Midlands of England), I wrote that the noise and glow from the blast furnace were like a night light and a cradle song. I gave these memories to the old man in the story. I doubt that I would ever have written these things down if I had not come to Western Australia. On arrival in a new country, a sense of place has to be established by a scrutiny of previous places in comparison with the present one.

I never thought of myself as a migrant. But migration, the travelling, the state of chosen exile has given me the feeling of inhabiting several worlds. Though the same language is spoken here there are colloquial differences. The climate and the customs and the clothes are different. The bright light and the blue skies in Western Australia made all our clothes seem very shabby. In Scotland, where we lived before changing countries, the doors and

windows along the street were kept closed winter and summer. Curtains and blinds covered the windows – but not to keep out the sun in Glasgow! In Western Australia, all along Parkway, the little street of houses on campus at the University, there were always women and children moving on the grass verges, in and out of each other's gardens and in and out of each other's houses, constantly visiting and exchanging children and dishes and recipes, the doors behind the fly screens always open, winter and summer. The greengrocer who came to Parkway with his van uttered the famous words: 'Whichever house you go to in this street, the same woman always comes to the door.'

The writer is often loyal to the landscape through attachment. In 1821 John Clare's publisher, John Taylor, moved by the descriptions in a recently published volume of Clare's, decided to visit the region described. He asked Clare to show him the places. On seeing them Taylor could only stare at Clare with amazement; *there was nothing but a dull line of ponds, or rather one continued marsh, over which a succession of arches carries the narrow highway.* The landscape has to be seen with the poet's eyes. The special quality is often in the loyalty and love that the writer feels towards a particular landscape.

My landscape is not to be found on any map, unless it is all over several maps. It is created from truth, from light and shade and, without going beyond the bounds of possibility, it is created in the imagination. I am careful not to make mistakes. My rivers do not flow uphill.

There are little seams in fiction where the old and the new, the half-forgotten, the remembered, the understood and the misunderstood are pieced together. The faithfulness, the loyalty of the writer is often stretched, the seams might be vivid with stitching or blurred and indistinct, but the essence of the real is contained in the imaginative use of the material.

The German language is fortunate in that it has one noun, *Dichtung*, that encompasses all forms of imaginative writing, so there is no need to explain that what is said of poetry need not be confined to verse.

People often ask me if moving from one country to another has affected my writing: 'What would you have written if you had stayed in England?' My reply is that I have no idea. But what I do know is that, without being disloyal to my previous country, there are certain experiences and observations I would have missed if I had remained in England. Until I came to Western Australia I had no real conception of the importance of water and its effects in and on the earth. In a dry country, water – either the lack of it or sudden floods of it – can be uppermost in a person's mind. Once, when I was teaching in the remote townships and farms in the wheat belt, a farmer's wife described the effects water has on the appearance of a paddock. I quickly made a note, and later gave this passage to a character in *Two Men Running*, who is running in his imagination through the remembered landscape of his childhood:

'The gravel pits, the hills, the catchment and the foxgloves in the catchment. Did you know,' I ask him, 'did you know that where the water collects and runs off the rocks there are different flowers growing there? Did you know that, because of this water, a paddock can be deep purple like a plum? And then, if you think about plums, the different colours range from deep purple through to the pale pearly green of the translucent satsuma before it ripens. Because of water that's how a paddock can look from one end to the other. It's the same with people . . .'

In writing this, I was trying to show something of my character's need to re-create for himself the wholesomeness of this remembered landscape. He is consoled, as indeed I have come to understand the earth is consoled, by the gift of water – providing it is not too much water.

The ability to make changes and to accept the differences, to be at home in the new country, depends on the development of the person in the country of origin. Forced exile is intolerable for most people. Chosen exile is not easy. For the writer, the difficulties of exile may well be of use for the memory and the feeling

and the imagination. James Joyce, in exile in France, filled his pages with Dublin. D. H. Lawrence, in search of clean air for his diseased lungs, tried to embrace new landscapes in his fiction, but he is at his best in the neighbourhood of lace-making factories, coal mines, colliers' cottages and the draughty vicarage drawing rooms around Nottingham.

Perhaps there is a kind of loyalty in the fact that here I have taken examples from my earlier background reading and have presented writers who are not only from another country, but from another age. If there are influences in a writer's life these may be seen, in later years, to come from earlier reading and study.

I want to say something about the writer's loyalty towards an observation, something which may have been seen or noticed in childhood and kept faithfully all the years. The power of observation, which is keen in childhood, persists in painters, writers and doctors (and others too, though it may be dissipated). Having made an observation, the human individual has the great gift of being able to store the experience. In the storehouse of the mind, a painter may keep an endless inventory – clouds and sunsets, the shapes and sizes of buildings, the expressions on people's faces, the colours of fruits and vegetables. The writer has this ability, too. The writer might store something that others have noticed but never fully described. The writer faithfully, with loyalty to his observation, finds the exact words and phrases to communicate something that could not be communicated in a phrase of music or by paint brush and colours. Let me try to show you what I mean. In the story 'The Grasshopper's Burden', by William Goyen (b. Texas 1915, d. 1983), the author describes a deformed and retarded boy, George Kurunus, who spends his life on the edge of the lives of the other children at his school. The outward attitude of the children is described first. One of the girls is on her way to a rehearsal of the school pageant:

. . . she suddenly heard someone coming down the hall and looked to see

who could it be. It was the awful deformity George Kurunus writhing and slobbering and skulking towards her. She was afraid of him and thought she would scream as all the girls did when he came to them; but she knew if you went up to him not afraid of his twisted face and said George to him and talked to him he would not do anything to you. Together, all the kids played with him, at him, as though he was some crazy and funny thing like a bent toy on a string; but no one ever wanted to be with him alone. Often a class would hear a scratching at the door and would see his hoodlum face at a door pane like Hallowe'en and be frightened until they saw it was just George Kurunus. Then the class would laugh and make faces back at him and the teacher would go to the door and say 'Now, George . . .' and shoo him away; and the class would titter. The boys all went around with him as if he was something they owned, something they could use for some stunt or trick on somebody, their arms around his shoulder . . .

That is the outward observation. The next quotation demonstrates what happens when the writer is showing the inward observation in a meticulous and convincing prose. Look again at the boy, George Kurunus:

Why did this deformity George have to be in a school? He couldn't even hold a word still in his mouth when he said it, for it rattled or hopped away – this was why he was in Stuttering Class, but it did him no good, he still broke a word when he said it, as if it were a twig, he still said ruined words.

He could not speak a word right and whole no matter how hard he tried or how carefully. But if you live among breakage, he may have reasoned, you finally see the wisdom in pieces; and no one can keep you from the pasting and joining together of bits to make the mind's own whole. What can break anything set back whole upon a shelf in the mind, like a mended dish? His mind, then, was full of mended words, broken by his own speech but repaired by his silences and put back into his mind. The wisdom in all things, in time, tells a meaning to those things, even to parcels of things that seem to mean disuse and no use, like scraps in a mending basket that are tokens and remnants of many splendid dresses and robes each with a whole to tell about.

Whenever the Twirling Class for girls in the Black and Gold Battalion practiced on the football field, here was this George on the field, too, like some old stray dog that had to be shooed away. And in a marching line of some class to somewhere, the library or a program in the auditorium, he ruined any straight marching line and so was put last to keep the line straight. But at the end of a straight marching line he twisted and wavered like the raveling out of a line and ruined it, even then; he was the capricious conclusion, and mocking collapse of something all ordered and precise right up to the end. When he walked, it seemed he always ran upon himself like someone in the way – or like a wounded insect. He was a flaw in the school, as if he were a crack in the building . . .

The two passages from the story, so fluently and perfectly written, are a pleasure to read. If they had not been written with sympathetic faithfulness and with carefully chosen words the writer might only have succeeded in producing an ugly truth without the added depths brought to the description by insight, tenderness and understanding.

The writer has to choose the best way for the characters in the novel or the story to speak. Weekly, one of the characters in my novel *The Newspaper of Claremont Street*, uses a modified idiom from the Black Country. The idiom is modified because she has been away from there for most of her life. For me, the writer, this was the best form of expression for her. When I created the character, the pronunciation and use of phrases I had long forgotten came back easily. This could be described as loyalty to the idiom of childhood. And if the writer has the mixed blessing of a foreign language spoken in the household of childhood, there is the broken language of more than one culture to fall back upon. Critics must be wary: in Australia there are now so many idiomatic backgrounds that what may seem like a faulty or an uneasy ear for the vernacular may in fact be a very accurate ear for the modifications of the vernacular brought here from the different parts of the world.

It seems more like good fortune than actual loyalty or faithful-

ness when a memory surfaces just at the right moment for a passage in a novel or a short story. My novel *Milk and Honey* contains the remembered shadows and the weeping of people my mother and father tried to help before and during the Second World War. Many refugees from Europe came to our house, and often my sister and I slept on the floor because these people, forced exiles, needed our beds.

Sometimes a childhood memory becomes suddenly vivid and powerful without it being written down. One of these was a game that my father described to me when I was about six years old. He and his sister, when they were children, played a game called horses and carts. They played on the kitchen table with an assortment of screws and nails and small nuts and bolts. The table was the street and the nuts and bolts and things went up and down, to and fro, fast and slow on the table. They were the horses and carts. In between games the screws and nails and the nuts and bolts were kept in a jar with a screw-top lid. More than fifty years later, having the sound of the game suddenly in my head – dot-dot-dotty-dot, as the screws and nails tapped along the table – I gave the game to a character:

We're running still, lightly now, one-foot-two-foot-one-foot-two-foot-foot-foot-breathe out breathe in. Side by side we're running, easily.

'What about the kitchen table?' he asks me. 'Where did you put your nuts and bolts?' His breathing's easier. 'Where'd you put yer horses and carts of a night time?'

'I knew you'd ask that,' I say. 'I'll tell you. My Dad made me a bit of a table out of an old box in the trailer and every night I set out my horses and carts, dot-dot-dotty-dot up and down, to and fro along the road, fast and slow, my horses and carts passed each other, stopped to let each other go by, they turned in the roadway and sometimes they collided.'

The boy in 'Two Men Running' plays this game while his father looks on. The progress of the game parallels some of the events and action in the story. I cannot explain why I should, at the right moment, remember this game. My sister, who is about a year

younger than I am, has no memory at all of the game being described.

It would seem that all writers draw heavily on their early experiences but in different ways. It would be interesting to know to what extent migration causes people to look back to events and customs in childhood. Tolstoy, Wordsworth, Traherne are examples of writers who recall and use childhood experience, Gorky and Dickens too (one might imagine that both Gorky and Dickens would have obliterated all memory of their childhood!).

But none of these writers migrated from one country to another. Samuel Johnson does not appear to write about or from his childhood experience. His 'migration' was from Lichfield in the Midlands to London. His legacy from infancy was an illness. Thomas Mann and Isaac Bashevis Singer are writers who left their native countries for America, and both include their own early experience in their writing. It is impossible to draw general conclusions.

Loyalty to our beginnings is essential. It is important to remember the aspects of the personality that Macbeth holds in the palm of his hand:

Who can be wise, amazed, temperate and furious,
Loyal and neutral, in a moment? No man . . .

Perhaps on coming to a new country the individual makes a special effort to succeed, to seek justification perhaps for making the great change. This effort is carried out with a certain amount of caution, for all human individuals (like animals) fear the stab in the back. Dogs turn round and round, treading a circle for their size, as if checking all the hollows in the cave for a hidden enemy before lying down to rest. They do this even in the safest places – the hearth rug before a comfortable fire. Perhaps in checking the hollows in the strange cave the traveller protects himself with details from his origins.

For a time the migrant feels that life is temporary in the new country. Partly unpacked trunks and boxes remain partly un-

packed. Certain things surface later, like many things forgotten. A road map of Birmingham discovered years later has a disturbing effect. The streets of Birmingham are not outside the front door of the house in Claremont.

Judah Waten, in his book *Alien Son*, has the best description of the landscape of migration:

Wherever we lived there were some cases partly unpacked, rolls of linoleum stood in a corner, only some of the windows had curtains. There were never sufficient wardrobes, so that clothes hung on hooks behind doors. And all the time Mother's things accumulated. She never parted with anything, no matter how old it was. A shabby green plush coat bequeathed to her by her own mother hung on a nail in her bedroom. Untidy heaps of tattered books, newspapers, and journals from the old country mouldered in corners of the house, while under her bed in tin trunks she kept her dearest possessions. In those trunks there were bundles of old letters, two heavily underlined books on nursing, an old Hebrew Bible, three silver spoons given her by an aunt with whom she had once lived, a diploma on yellow parchment, and her collection of favourite books.

But then there is the stab, the hole in the teapot that seemed like treachery, like the stab one person can give another. I say the hole *seemed* treacherous for I quickly discovered that even teapots carry a little of the herb of self heal. Mine healed itself. It repaired itself with its own tea leaves. Perhaps the writer in writing can close the spaces, can console and heal others and in this heal himself.

Fay Weldon edits herself

I used to implore apprentice writers to avoid adjectives, until one of them snarkily pointed out that Iris Murdoch is capable of writing sixteen adjectives in a row and it works wonderfully . . . A 'weakness', I now realize, is nothing but a strength not properly developed.

Fay Weldon is a novelist, short-story writer and television dramatist. Her novels, which have been translated throughout the world, include *Female Friends*, *The Cloning of Joanna May* and *The Life and Loves of a She Devil*, which she adapted both for television and the Hollywood screen. Her latest novel is *Life Force*.

HARNESSED TO THE HARPY

NOTES FOR ASPIRING WRITERS

From first to final draft

or

Thinking aloud on re-drafting

Para 1 Forget, for the time being, *why* you're writing what you are, let alone *what* you're writing – for those are other ballgames – forget the characters you are inventing (with any luck) or describing (if you're reduced to it) who will inhabit this text of yours: forget the internal or external landscape within which you have set these characters, let alone the journey you have sent them upon – for that

Para 1.5 too is another ballgame – and just for the moment shall we consider the perfect expression of all these things: the way the writer actually sets words upon the page to represent, as simply and gracefully as she or he can, the train of thought which goes on inside the writer's head and which the writer intends by means of the written word, to transfer into the head of a perfect stranger.

Para 2 That sentence is in first draft. The first half's okay – the second half's rotten. The whole goes on for 139 words, which is neither here nor there. The sentence which follows it did its work in six words. Okay, so there's variety for you, and don't think because a sentence is short and looks easy it's going to be simpler to handle. The more sentences you take to say what you mean the more closely each has to relate to what went before and what comes next; the intricacies of sequence can be a real problem. (Do you mean 'Yet' when you find you've said 'But', or should it be 'However'?) Writing *is* a problem and, what's more, it's hard work. When I re-

read the opening sentence, I begin to get annoyed with it after eight lines – if I get annoyed with it (and it's mine) how much sooner will a stranger resent it? So I shall have to redraft it, make alterations. I have to admit error. That can be hard too. *Mea culpa*. The words which crept down the page easily enough, no longer represented exactly what I wanted to say. Language had taken over from meaning. They sounded okay, just about, as I allowed them to drift out of my head and my hand moved my pen to produce them, but they don't stand up to close inspection. I had lost, as they say, my train of thought. Look at it like this: the train had moved out of the station and I was running after it, and couldn't catch up: so I have to back it into the station and start over – and the passengers aren't half complaining about the delay – 'Let's get on,' they're crying. 'Just can't we get on with it?' No. We have to go back and it's boring.

Para 3   And then consider, would-be writer, that if I, who have been writing for years, still have to carry on in this way, drafting and redrafting, refining and elaborating, searching for proper expression, whether this sort of thing is really how you wish to spend your life. The rewards are often negligible: it's a hideously personal kind of thing you're doing. You are working upon the inside of your head to make what's in there comprehensible to others. And, what is more, what is worse, you must be prepared to do as adults what children so hate doing; that is to say, read your work *aloud* before you hand it in.

Para 4   But let me first give you a facsimile A of what the first page looked like as I tried to get it together; before it had even been typed:

How To Get From Here to There: ...

Forget, for the time being, ~~why~~ who you're writing what you are, n what you're writing, n ~~the~~ ~~the characters~~, n the story, n ~~the landscape~~ people you are inventing (well any level) n describing (if you're reduced to it) n the ~~/~~ landscape you have ~~sent~~ them in, n the journey you have sent them ~~on, n they get from here to there, either is~~ you, n the wish and turns of plot, shall we just for the moment consider the expansion of ~~these~~ these things: the ~~language you employ~~ words which you ~~set~~ set upon the ~~train of~~ page to represent, as gracefully as you can, the ~~thoughts~~ when your head, which you, by this strange ~~means~~, intend to plant within the head of someone else — shall we say, the reader?

That sentence was the trick dealt. It contains 130 words, and goes to pieces towards the end, which was probably when you, the reader, began to be annoyed with it. ~~The word was~~ It was no longer representing ~~they sounded strong, just about, we never harden, stand up to inspection~~ exactly what I wanted to say, I had lost my own train of thought. ~~It was not what I~~ ~~So I was re-reading~~ On re-reading, it ~~meaning seemed precise enough~~ precise enough until ~~these~~ things, ~~which~~ ~~suggestion~~ ~~to put the~~? ~~other things~~ these ~~is in the first 87 words.~~ So put a query after 'things' and let me try again from there.

And let me give you a facsimile of what this first page looks like as I try to get it together. And then remember I have been ~~writing~~ on a computer and still have to carry on either then, ~~have to solve it, and to say,~~ redrafting, refining n salvaging, carding the proper expression; ~~so let me not put you off, let me put...~~ ~~but you must be prepared to do...~~ ~~to...~~ ~~so hate doing, learn to say, read your work aloud...~~ things are possible in writing in long as you get away and it.

Para 5   Now you're looking at facsimile A please notice how the words get squashed up towards the end. I suspect this is because I fear I'll lose the flow if I turn the page. But how do I know what my real motives were? If you're me you write first, think later. I am aware that what I have said so far may be counterindicative of 'flow'. (Now that's awful: 'Counterindicative of flow'! I'll have to take the whole sentence out. This thing is getting so involved already, the less of it there is the better. When in doubt, cut! It probably doesn't even exist as a word and if it does it shouldn't: it will have some soulless Roman root. On the whole the short words of Saxon or Celtic origin are easier to throw around, go more quickly to the heart ... Where was I? Ah, within a bracket – let me get out of it.) I was talking about 'flow'. (Horrible word anyhow.) If the words you write down on the page are to end up carrying meaning you hardly rationally comprehend yourself, are to elucidate ideas you are barely conscious of, why then 'flow' is required.

Para 6   Now let's investigate that last sentence. Dreadful. What do I *mean* 'elucidate ideas I am barely conscious of'? Forget 'elucidate' being another Roman word – *elucido*: to make clear – forget it ought to be 'of which you are barely conscious' – it just *sounds* phoney. That means it probably is. Investigate the self that wrote it. What am I trying to say, I ask myself, as I bring that last sentence-paragraph to its too neat, too literary conclusion? That the act of writing pre-empts, as it were, the substance of what is written? I fear so. (Do I really believe that? If I wrote it I probably believe it. In the end, if you keep covering the pages decade after decade, as I do, you begin to discover what went on in your head by reading what you have written. The phenomena were not apparent when I began writing. Beginners, alas, have to

think first, write next. Poor beginners!) Then I must attempt, now I know what I mean, to say all this in a more convincing manner than I managed in the last lines of Para 5. To this end I will strike the whole lot out and write it again. There now, that's done.

Para 7   But, but – something niggles. Yes. The ideas in Para 1; the second part of the overlong sentence: I left all that in the air, didn't I?

Para 8   Para 1.5 went (originally) like this – before I overedited it, adding some 25 words in a foolish attempt to be explicit. It was better in its first version, (see facsimile A):

'Forget, for the time being, why you're writing what you are, let alone what you're writing; forget the characters you are inventing (with any luck) or describing (if you're reduced to it) to people this work; forget the internal or external landscape you have set these characters in, let alone the journey you have sent them upon, that is to say the twists and turns of plot as they get from here to there, and shall we just for a moment consider the expression of all these things?'

I was right to stop the sentence at 'things?' and start a new one. I'll go back to that version, before I heavied it up and ruined it by interfering with it.

Para 9   After 'things?' it would make more sense if I simply said (Para 1.5), 'All the writer has at his or her command is words, to get what is in the head into the reader's head, and the more precisely, the more economically, and the more convincingly you deal with these words, the more effective you will be in your purpose. And the more rapidly you will develop the mysterious and desirable quality called "style".'

Para 10   Forget everything between Paras 1.5 to 9 inclusive – perhaps it could *all* be cut – and let's get on with style.

'Style' is not something to be consciously sought after: it arrives by itself, if you ask me, at some moment between the first and the final draft. I couldn't define it. It has something to do, I think, with the proportion that exists between what the writer wishes to say, and the economy of language with which he or she manages to say it. The writer makes his writing as simple as possible, given the complexity of whatever it is that he or she is determined to express. Writers have any number of different things to say and work out their own way of saying it; all styles are different, as all handwritings are different, and the better the writer, the more recognizable the style. Pick up a good novel at random – open it – oh yes, that's Dickens, or that's Amis, father or son, or that one's Graham Greene. You know it at once, though *how* you know you'd be hard put to tell any more than you can say *how* you recognize a face. And there aren't any rules to learn and so ease the task, though people will keep telling me there are. I used to implore apprentice writers to avoid adjectives, until one of them snarkily pointed out that Iris Murdoch is capable of writing sixteen adjectives in a row and it works wonderfully. So I changed my tune. A 'weakness', I now realize, is nothing but a strength not properly developed. Take it to extremes and it works. It might strike some as a 'weakness' not to bother about using capital letters, but the poet e.e. cummings did well enough by simply not. That's why the 'teaching' of writing is such a problem. There is no proper way to do it – it's just that the reader shouldn't be conscious that the words upon the page ever presented the writer with a problem. But all that's by the by. My purpose in writing this piece is to suggest ways of getting from here to there, of how to travel from first to final draft. I have been thinking aloud and getting into a fine confusing mess. But I have a plan for those of you who

have bravely struggled on this far: and by so doing have shown patience, perseverance, and the will to accomplish great things in the face of difficulty. These qualities you will need if you persist in your plan to be a writer.

When B met A

Para 11 I once, some years ago, and for the purposes of writing yet another article about writing, split myself into a number of personalities: in my then theory of self, the master personality, X, was the writer, and decidedly male: Y was the housewife/mother; there were a number of other splitting-offs, L and M, N and R, I called them, all more or less delinquent. X knew all about the other personalities and controlled them, even getting Y into trouble via the other personalities for the purposes of getting copy. Y knew nothing about L, M, N and R, let alone X, and lived in a perpetual state of anxiety. She was an amiable, messy, languid creature, forever surprised at the number of carefully written pages which kept turning up on the kitchen table. She had no recollection of having written them, and no idea, when asked, how she found the time to accomplish them amongst her various household tasks.

Para 12 These days I'd more subtly divide X into two personalities – A and B. A is the one who produces the first drafts: A is creative, impetuous, wilful, emotional, sloppy: she works by hand. B does the editing – works from the printout, achieves the subsequent drafts and is argumentative, self-righteous, cautious, rational, effective, perfectionist, ambitious. I'm not sure about the gender of either – A is on the whole female, B male, but they do switch and swap. Both are strong personalities: both are in perpetual argument one with the other, but are only truly happy

when in accord, hand in hand. They're fighting it out this very moment in a small hotel room in Gottingen, in Germany.

Para 13   B is currently looking over what A has been writing: if B (who suspects he has flu) was feeling stronger he would instruct A to indeed delete everything between Para 1.5 and Para 11 but he's alone in a foreign land with a headache and A, who is feeling stroppy and self-indulgent and perfectly healthy, is strongly defending these paragraphs, not wanting to see anything wasted. B sees whimsy at the end of Para 10, A's saying, 'Too bad! Leave it in!' All B can reply is, 'No one's going to read all that; it's much too obscure: would-be writers, A, may indeed be interested in what goes on in writers' heads but you take it too far. Para 1.5 to Para 10 was only the base of the iceberg which is the article: you had to write in all that junk, I acknowledge, in order to find out what you meant, but it's what appears above the water line that counts; what's below is not the reader's business.' A really mustn't break the cardinal rule – that is to say oblige the reader to bear witness to his/her pains. Besides, Para 1.5 to Para 10 are going to come over sleazy and somehow self-congratulating. Get rid of them or, failing that, go back to the original draft of Para 1 (see Para 8).

    'To hell with all that,' replies A. 'Take an aspirin and go away. What's done is done. Everything stays!' adding, knowing that this kind of thing sends B into paroxysms of outrage, 'Do you know how little I'm getting paid for writing this? I'm going off to have a cup of coffee. You can just stuff it, B.' B never thinks about money: A often does. You'd think it would be the other way round, but no. B's the one with the integrity.

Para 14   But, serve A right, there is no coffee: unless she is prepared to find her shoes, her door key, use her lipstick

and go downstairs, and ask for *ein Kaffee* in German. The reason that A and B are cooped up together in this small hotel room is that, at the request of the British Council, they are to join forces this evening to talk to readers; 'readers' being a concept A and B, when they are on speaking terms, will refer to as 'C'. C is understood to exist, as a class, as a by-product of A and B, which is why A and B both feel they have a duty towards C and will travel long and inconvenient distances to fulfil it, even as A will put up with receiving almost no money at all.

'You go down for coffee,' says B to A. 'I'll stay up here and think.'

'There's no fun in that,' says A. 'If you don't come with me I can't *see* anyone, let alone taste the coffee: I'll trip over, lose my glasses, or forget to pay. What kind of life is this, anyway? It's unnatural. For God's sake, come with me, let me just have a cup of coffee like anyone else –'

Para 15 But still B refuses to come, so, once A has located her room key, which she needs to open the mini-fridge, they stay in the room and share a Diet Coke. It is a pleasant room, albeit small. Across the autumnal square A and B can see the railway station and look forward to their departure. Not that they didn't have fun. They went out together earlier and bought some German paper to write upon and some German pens to write with. They like to confer upon matters of stationery. Different nations produce very different stationery, they observe. English writing pads have somehow chalkier, more absorbent surfaces than those produced in the rest of Europe. A likes broader, softer pens than does B, who favours fine pens, the better to take A's work from its first to its final draft. A and B enjoy these outings to stationery shops

abroad, for at these times they are more or less in accord, and feel permitted to buy as many pens as they want, although the wretched A is sometimes taken to task for talking aloud in shops. She has no idea that she's doing it. A is the one people see. B keeps invisible.

'Tell you what,' concedes B when the aspirin has taken care of her headache, 'I'll let you keep in Paras 2 to 10 if you put in something simple and helpful and to the brief.' So what A, who knows she has pushed her luck, and giving up hope of being allowed to take time off for coffee, does, is to put in the first draft of the opening paragraphs of a story by one Janice Marriott, a New Zealand writer of children's books who is now branching out into adult fiction. This is how it runs in its first draft.

Para 16   *The Woman Who Flew*

The day before Bea flew started routinely with her cat Jellicle patting Bea's face at 6.30, and Bea pretending Jellicle was a very understanding man asking her if she wanted to have coffee and croissants. 'Oh, thank you, Jolyon. Just half a croissant would be heaven.' And then he said he'd fix the gutterings and top the confounded macrocarpa next door which cut out her afternoon sun, and she said the neighbour mightn't like it, and he hummed 'Who cares?' and then pushed his hummy be-whiskered self against her nose and said he'd fight to the death for her, his unique princess Bea. Jellicle pushed the edges of his mouth against her cheek and dribbled, and that really was too much for Bea. She turned the duvet back just enough. Another working day rose up to meet her tentative feet.

She showered and reviewed the day's meetings and

what she wanted to achieve in each. She wrapped her dressing-gown round herself, and creamed her face thickly with Vitamin E anti-wrinkle cream. As always, Jellicle waited beside the fridge. While he ate, Bea turned on the radio and plugged in the jug which she always kept half full, just enough for a small pot of tea. 'Here is the news, read by . . .' It pleased her every day that her timing was so perfect.

Para 17 On reading the beginning of this story by the Janice Marriott, A, the Weldon, B, who is an interfering harpy, took up her pen and started interfering. This is what she did.

Para 18 *The Woman Who Flew*

The day ~~before~~ Bea flew started **as usual, the** ~~routinely with her~~ cat Jellicle patt**ed** ~~ing~~ Bea's face at 6.30, and Bea pretend**ed** ~~ing~~ Jellicle was ~~a very~~ **an** understanding man asking her**, Bea,** if she **would like** ~~wanted to have~~ coffee and croissants. ~~Oh~~ 'Thank you, Jolyon**; replied Bea. &** ~~Just~~ half **a** croissant would be heaven.' ~~And then~~ **The understanding man watched her eat and told her** ~~he said~~ he'd fix the gutterings and top the ~~confounded~~ macrocarpa next door which cut out **the** ~~her~~ afternoon sun, and **when Bea** ~~she~~ said the neighbour mightn't like it, ~~and~~ he hummed 'Who cares?' ~~and~~ Then **he** pushed his hummy be- whiskered self against **Bea's** ~~her~~ nose and said he'd fight to the

(margin note:) Just small things, but to do with precision of expression and getting the time sequence accurate

death for her, ~~his unique~~ *the* princess Bea. *But then the cat went too far and* Jellicle pushed the

edges of his mouth against ~~her~~ *Bea's* cheek and dribbled, and

that ~~really was too much for Bea. She~~ *could no longer be ignored. So* turned the duvet

to change the understanding man into the cat Jellicle. back just enough. Another working day rose up to meet

~~her~~ *Bea's* tentative feet.

While Bea ~~She~~ showered and reviewed the day's meetings, and

~~when~~ *the various things* she wanted to achieve in ~~each.~~ *every one of them.* She wrapped her

dressing-gown round herself, and creamed her face

thickly with Vitamin E anti-wrinkle cream. ~~As always,~~ *, as was his custom,*

Jellicle waited beside the fridge. ~~While he ate~~ *until his breakfast came.* Bea turned *provided it, and then*

on the radio and plugged in the jug which she always

kept half full, *of water,* just enough for a small pot of tea. *when it boiled she heard the radio say* 'Here is

Every day she was the news, read by . . .' ~~It~~ pleased ~~her every day~~ that her

timing was so perfect.

So that the paragraphs, the corrections incorporated, now read thus:

Para 19 The day Bea flew started as usual. The cat Jellicle patted Bea's face at 6.30, and Bea pretended Jellicle was an understanding man asking her, Bea, if she would like coffee and croissants. 'Thank you, Jolyon,' replied Bea.

'Just a half croissant would be heaven.' The understanding man watched her eat, and then told her he'd fix the gutterings and top the macrocarpa next door which cut out the afternoon sun, and when Bea said the neighbour mightn't like it, he hummed 'Who cares?' Then he pushed his hummy bewhiskered self against Bea's nose and said he'd fight to the death for her, the princess Bea. But then the cat Jellicle went too far and pushed the edges of his mouth against Bea's cheek and dribbled, and that could no longer be ignored. So Bea turned the duvet back just enough to change the understanding man back into Jellicle. Another working day rose up to meet Bea's tentative feet.

While Bea showered she reviewed the day's meetings, and the various things she wanted to achieve in every one of them. She wrapped her dressing-gown round herself, and creamed her face thickly with Vitamin E anti-wrinkle cream. Jellicle, as was his custom, waited beside the fridge until his breakfast came. Bea provided it, and then turned on the radio and plugged in the jug which she always kept half-full of water, just enough for a small pot of tea. When it boiled she heard the radio say, 'Here is the news, read by . . .' Every day she was pleased that her timing was so perfect.

Para 20 Because it's the Weldon B, not Janice Marriott's B, the paragraphs end up rather in the Weldon style, but once Ms Marriott's B is fully developed people will no doubt say, opening her latest book of stories, 'Oh yes, that's Janice Marriott.' All I can do is demonstrate to Ms Marriott the existence of B, curled so far foetus-like within her head, waiting to burst out and no doubt make her life a misery with the kind of endless arguments I have been describing, but making her work more instantly publishable and with any luck profitable.

'Okay,' A says to B, 'can I bring this piece to a conclusion now?'

'Oh no,' says B, made bad-tempered by the mention of profit, 'you mentioned C; we can't just leave C hanging in mid-air.'

'We can,' says A. 'No one will notice.'

That is the other statement that drives B mad. '*I* notice,' says B. 'That is all that counts,' so forcefully that A, who wants to try out the new Braun curling tongs she bought when B was already in anticipation grumbling and mumbling about felt tips versus rollerballs, desists, and goes into her party piece about C, the reader, writing on the smoothly surfaced, agreeable German A4 pad.

Para 21 'Look at it like this,' writes A. 'Writers write for readers, not publishers or critics, or friends, let alone loved ones. A and B stand together and it is their task to hurl this perfect object, this thing they have written, over a great obstacle, so it lands into the eager hands of the reader, C. The obstacle which stands in the way seems as high as a hill, stolid as a church, a lump of concrete, dense as the Chernobyl tomb, in which, flailing and wailing, are set agents, publishers, designers, booksellers, critics, literary pundits, marketing experts, censors and Arts councils, not to mention loved ones, all of whom sincerely believe they are helping you get your book where you want it to be, but never get it quite right. It is A and B's joint responsibility, no one else's, to render this thing perfect before it leaves their hands. A and B together must perform an intimate act of communication with C. A and B know instinctively what C responds to: otherwise publishers and all the rest would have done away with writers long ago, and put it all on computer. If the writer writes to please, let it at least be the reader, not the publisher

who is to be pleased, or the whole world will give up reading.'

Para 22   'If you drop an egg it breaks,' observes A to B, breaking off the writing. 'But if you hurl it over a house it will land at a certain angle and roll unbroken away. This is true. I have seen it done. Don't you remember, when we worked in advertising? I don't think I'd met you then.'

'Yes, yes,' says B. 'I was around some of the time in those days, and I saw it too, but what the fuck has this to do with anything? The analogy is nice but it isn't exact. It's indulgent. Anyway, it rambles. Cut it out. Excise it. Don't even let it get as far as the page!'

'What I am trying to say,' says A politely (radio gives the writer an allowance of one 'fuck' per 60 minutes in A's head, and B has somehow gone and used it up in advance: so A is *really* irritated), 'is that it's no use offering half-finished work to anyone lurking in the concrete block . . .' – 'For God's sake,' says B, 'people can't lurk in concrete blocks!' – '. . . hitherto described (Para 21) and asking for their opinion: they either don't have an opinion or they have too many: what do they know anyway? If they knew how to do it, they'd be writing themselves. Of course they'll all offer an opinion. They are paid to offer it, or else they're your boyfriend, girlfriend, spouse and/or parent whom you've rashly asked what they think of your work and now they have to reply, and of course they have a hidden agenda. All we know, A and B, is that we must deliver work to publishers that's as perfect as can be, in which we are in a position to argue for every word, every sentiment we have expressed because we have already argued it through with one another.'

Para 23   'Well, thanks,' says B, gratified, when A has managed to get that all down on paper, 'though personally I'm on

the side of the publishers' editors. The rubbish they have to contend with!'

Para 24 'Which does not mean,' writes A, obligingly, 'that you will refuse to do as the livers in the concrete suggest; they do, after all, wield the practical power: but the moral power is with the writer, so long, that is, as she/he remembers his duty, not just to C, but to the smooth perfection of the object that passes between writer and reader, and puts herself/himself subordinate to that.'

'Hang on a minute,' says B. 'Subordinate? Isn't that a bit Roman?'

'Oh shut up,' says A, 'that's enough. I'm going to curl my hair.'

Para 25 But A has to acknowledge she is nothing without B, or B without A. There are lots of would-be writers wandering around looking for their other halves. Unless they meet up, I fear they may well have had it.

BETTER AND SICKER

Lorrie Moore

Writing is both the excursion into and the excursion out of one's life. That is the queasy paradox of the artistic life. It is the thing that, like love, removes one both painfully and deliciously from the ordinary shape of existence.

BETTER AND SICKER

Recently I received a letter from an acquaintance in which he said, 'By the way, I've been following and enjoying your work. It's getting better: deeper and sicker.'

Because the letter was handwritten, I convinced myself, for a portion of the day, that perhaps the last word was *richer*. But then I picked up the letter and looked at the word again: there was the *s*, there was the *k*. There was no denying it. Even though denial had been my tendency of late. I had recently convinced myself that a note I'd received from an ex-beau (in what was a response to my announcement that I'd gotten married) had read 'Best Wishes for Oz'. I considered this an expression of bitterness on my ex-beau's part, a snide lapse, a doomed man's view of marriage, and it gave me great satisfaction. *Best Wishes for Oz*. Eat your heart out, I thought. You had your chance. Cry me a river. Later a friend, looking at the note, pointed out that, Look: this isn't an O. This is a nine – see the tail? And this isn't a Z. This is a 2. This says 92. 'Best wishes for 92.' It hadn't been cryptic bitterness at all – only an indifferent little New Year's greeting. How unsatisfying!

So now when I looked at *deeper and richer*, I knew I had to be careful not to misread wishfully. The phrase wasn't, finally, *deeper and richer*; it was deeper and *sicker*. My work was deeper and sicker.

But what did that mean, *sicker*, and why or how might this adjective be applied in a friendly manner? I wasn't sure. But it brought me to thinking of the things that I had supposed fiction was supposed to be, what art was supposed to be, what writers

and artists were supposed to do, and whether it could possibly include some aesthetics of sickness.

I think it's a common thing for working writers to go a little blank when asking themselves too many fundamental questions about what it is they're doing. Some of this has to do with the lost perspective that goes with being so immersed. And some of it has to do with just plain not having a clue. Of course, this is the curse of the grant application, for instance, which includes that hilarious part called the project description (describe in detail the book you are going to write) wherein you are asked to know the unknowable, and if not to know it then just to say it anyway for cash. That a grant-giving agency would trust a specific and detailed description from a fiction writer seems sweetly naive – though fiction writers are also allowed to file their own taxes, write their own parents, sign their own checks, raise their own children – so it is a tolerant and generous or at least innocent world here and there.

What writers do is workmanlike: tenacious, skilled labour. That we know. But it is also mysterious. And the mystery involved in the act of creating a narrative is attached to the mysteries of life itself, and the creation of life itself: that we are; that there is *something* rather than *nothing*. Though I wonder whether it sounds preposterous in this day and age to say such a thing. No one who has ever looked back upon a book she or he has written, only to find the thing foreign and alienating, unrecallable, would ever deny this mysteriousness. One can't help but think that in some way this surprise reflects the appalled senility of God herself, or himself, though maybe it's the weirdly paired egotism and humility of artists that leads them over and over again to this creational cliché: that we are God's dream, God's characters; that literary fiction is God's compulsion handed down to us, an echo, a diminishment, but something we are made to do in imitation, perhaps even in honour, of that original creation, and made to do in understanding of what flimsy vapours we all are – though also

how heartbreaking and amusing. In more scientific terms, the compulsion to read and write – and it seems to me it should be, even must be, a compulsion – is a bit of mental wiring the species has selected, over time, in order, as the life span increases, to keep us interested in ourselves.

For it's crucial to keep ourselves, as a species, interested in ourselves. When that goes, we tip into the void, we harden to rock, we blow away and disappear. Art has been given to us to keep us interested and engaged – rather than distracted by material-ism or sated with boredom – so that we can attach to this life, a life which might, otherwise, be an unbearable one.

And so, perhaps, it is this compulsion to keep ourselves interested that can make the work seem, well, a little sick. (I'm determined, you see, if not to read *sicker* as *richer* then at least to read *sicker* as *OK*.) Certainly so much of art originates and locates itself within the margins, that is, the contours, of the human self, as a form of locating and defining that self. And certainly art, and the life of the artist, requires a goodly amount of shamelessness. The route to truth and beauty is a toll road – tricky and unpretty in and of itself.

But are the impulses toward that journey pathological ones?

I took inventory of my own life.

Certainly as a child, I had done things that now seem like clues indicating I was headed for a life that was not quite normal – one that was perhaps 'artistic'. I detached things: the charms from bracelets, the bows from dresses. This was a time – the early sixties, an outpost, really, of the fifties – when little girls' dresses had lots of decorations: badly stitched appliqué, or little plastic berries, lace flowers, satin bows. I liked to remove them and would often then re-attach them – on a sleeve or a mitten. I liked to re-contextualize even then – one of the symptoms. Other times, I would just collect these little detached things and play with them, keeping them in a little bowl in a dresser drawer in my room. If my dresses had been denuded, made homely, it didn't

matter to me: I had a supply of lovely little gew-gaws in a bowl. I had begun a secret life. A secret harvest. I had begun perhaps a kind of literary life – one that would continue to wreak havoc on my wardrobe, but, alas, those are the dues. I had become a magpie, collecting shiny objects. I was a starling in reverse: building a nest under eggs gathered from here and there.

When I was a little older, say eleven or twelve, I used to sit on my bed with a sketch pad, listening to songs on the radio. Each song would last three to four minutes, and during that time, I would draw the song: I would draw the character I imagined was singing the song, and the setting that character was in – usually there were a lot of waves and seagulls, docks and coastlines. I lived in the mountains, away from the ocean, but a babysitter I'd had when I was nine had taught me how to draw lighthouses, so I liked to stick in a lighthouse whenever possible. After one song was over, I'd turn the page and draw the next one, filling notebooks this way. I was obsessed with songs – songs and letters (I had a pen-pal in Canada) – and I often think that that is what I tried to find later in literature: the feeling of a song; the friendly, confiding voice of a letter but the cadence and feeling of a song. When a piece of prose hit rhythms older, more familiar and enduring than itself, it seemed then briefly to belong to nature, or at least to the world of music, and that's when it seemed to me 'artistic' and good.

I exhibited other signs of a sick life – a strange, elaborate crush on Bill Bixby, a belief in a fairy godmother, also a bit of journalism my brother and I embarked on called Mad Man Magazine, which consisted of our writing on notebook paper a lot of articles we'd make up about crazy people, especially crazy people in haunted houses, then tying the pages together with ribbon and selling them to family members for a nickel. But it was a life of the imagination.

When I was older, I suppose there were other signs of sickness. I preferred hearing about parties to actually going to them. I liked to phone the next day and get the news from a friend. I wanted

gossip, third-handedness; narrative. My reading was scattered, random, unsystematic. I wasn't one of these nice teenaged girls who spent their summers reading all of Jane Austen. My favourite books were *The Great Gatsby* by F. Scott Fitzgerald and *Such Good Friends* by Lois Gould. Later, like so many (of the 'afflicted'), I discovered the Brontës. One enters these truly great, truly embarrassing books like a fever dream – in fact, fever dreams figure prominently in them. They are situated in sickness, and unafraid of that. And that's what made them wonderful to me. They were at the centre of something messy. But they didn't seem foreign in the least. In fact, very little written by a woman seemed foreign to me. Books by women came as great friends, a relief. They showed up on the front lawn and waved. Books by men one had to walk a distance to get to, take a hike to arrive at, though as readers we girls were all well-trained for the hike and we didn't learn to begrudge and resent it until later. A book by a woman, a book that began up close, on the heart's porch, was a treat, an exhilaration, and finally, I think, that is why women who became writers did so: to create more books in the world by women; to give themselves something more to read.

When I first started writing, I often felt sorry for men, especially white men, for it seemed the reasons for their becoming writers was not so readily apparent, or compelling, but had to be searched for, even made excuses for. Though their quote-unquote tradition was so much more celebrated and available, it was also more filled up. It was ablaze. What did a young male writer feel he was adding? As a woman, I never felt that. There seemed to be a few guiding lights (I, of course, liked the more demented ones – Sexton, Plath, McCullers), but that was enough. Admiration and enthusiasm and a sense of scarcity: inspiration without the anxiety of influence.

I feel a little less like that now, in part because I know the main struggle for every writer is with the dance and limitations of language – to honour the texture of it but also to make it unafraid. One must throw all that one is into language, like a Christmas

tree hurled into a pool. One must listen and proceed, sentence to sentence, hearing what comes next in one's story – which can be a little maddening. It can be like trying to understand a whisper in a foreign accent: did she say *Je t'adore* or *Shut the door*?

To make the language sing while it works is a task to one side of gender. How often I've tried to shake from my own storytelling the phrase *And then suddenly*, as if I could wake up a story with the false drama of those three words. It's usually how I know my writing's going badly; I begin every sentence that way: *And then suddenly he went to the store. And then suddenly the store was brick. And then suddenly he had been asleep for eight hours*. The writer marries the language, said Auden, and out of this marriage writing is born. But what if the language feels inadequate, timid, recalcitrant, afraid? I often think of the Albert Goldbarth poem 'Alien Tongue' wherein the poet thinks wistfully, adulterously of an imagined language parsed to such a thinness that there is a tense that means 'I would have if I'd been my twin'. What an exquisite, precision tool such a tense would be for a writer! Whole rooms could be added to scenes; whole paragraphs to pages; books to books; sequels where at first there were no sequels. . . . But then excessive literary production, George Eliot reminds us, is a social offence. As far as language goes we have to live contentedly, and discontentedly, with our own, making it do what it can, and also, a little of what it can't. And this contradiction brings one back, I suppose, to a makeshift aesthetics of sickness.

Writing is both the excursion into and the excursion out of one's life. That is the queasy paradox of the artistic life. It is the thing that, like love, removes one both painfully and deliciously from the ordinary shape of existence. It joins another queasy paradox: that life is both an amazing, hilarious, blessed gift and that it is also intolerable. Even in the luckiest life, for example, one loves someone and then that someone dies. This is not *acceptable*. This is a major design flaw! To says nothing of the world's truly calamitous lives. The imagination is meant outwardly to console

us with all that is interesting, not so much to subtract but to add to our lives. It reminds me of a progressive Italian elementary school I read of once in which the classrooms had two dress-up areas with trunks of costumes – just in case, while studying math or plants, a child wanted to be in disguise that day.

But the imagination also forces us inward. It constructs inwardly from what has entered our inwardness. The best art, especially literary art, embraces the very idea of paradox: it sees opposites, antitheses co-existing. It sees the blues and violets, in a painting of an orange; it sees the scarlets and the yellows in a bunch of Concord grapes. In narrative, tones share space – often queasily, the ironies quivering. Consider these lines from the Alice Munro story, 'A Real Life': 'Albert's heart had given out – he had only had time to pull to the side of the road and stop the truck. He died in a lovely spot, where black oaks grew in a bottomland, and a sweet, clear creek ran beside the road.' Or these lines from a Garrison Keillor monologue: 'And so he tasted it, and a look of pleasure came over him, and then he died. Ah, life is good. Life is good.' What constitutes tragedy and what constitutes comedy may be a fuzzy matter. The comedienne Joan Rivers has said that there isn't any suffering that's one's own that isn't also potentially very funny. Delmore Schwartz claimed that the only way anyone could understand *Hamlet* was to assume right from the start that all the characters were roaring drunk. I often think of an acquaintance of mine who is also a writer and whom I ran into once in a bookstore. We exchanged hellos, and when I asked her what she was working on these days, she said, 'Well, I *was* working on a long comic novel, but then in the middle of the summer my husband had a terrible accident with an electric saw and lost three of his fingers. It left us so sad and shaken that when I returned to writing, my comic novel kept getting droopier, darker and sadder and depressing. So I scrapped it, and started writing a novel about a man who loses three fingers in an accident with a saw, and *that*,' she said, '*that's* turning out to be really funny.'

A lesson in comedy.

Which leads one also to that paradox, or at least that paradoxical term 'autobiographical fiction'. Fiction writers are constantly asked, is this autobiographical? Book reviewers aren't asked this; and neither are concert violinists, though, in my opinion, there is nothing more autobiographical than a book review or a violin solo. But because literature has always functioned as a means by which to figure out what is happening to us, as well as what we think about it, fiction writers do get asked: 'What is the relationship of this story/novel/play to the events of your own life (whatever they may be)?'

I do think that the proper relationship of a writer to his or her own life is similar to a cook with a cupboard. What that cook makes from what's in the cupboard is not the same thing as what's in the cupboard – and of course, everyone understands that. Even in the most autobiographical fiction there is a kind of *paraphrase*, going on, which is Katherine Anne Porter's word, and which is a good one for use in connection with her, but also for general use. I personally have never written autobiographically in the sense of using and transcribing events from my life. None – or at least very few – of the things that have happened to my characters have ever happened to me. But one's life is there constantly collecting and providing and it will creep into one's work regardless – in emotional ways. I often think of a writing student I had once who was blind. He never once wrote about a blind person – never wrote about blindness at all. But he wrote about characters who constantly bumped into things, who tripped, who got bruised; and that seemed to me a very true and very characteristic transformation of life into art. He wanted to imagine a person other than himself; but his journey toward that person was *paradoxically* and necessarily through his own life. Like a parent with children, he gave his characters a little of what he knew – but not everything. He nurtured rather than replicated or transcribed.

Autobiography can be a useful tool: it coaxes out the invention – actually invention and autobiography coax out each other; the

pen takes refuge from one in the other, looking for moral dignity and purpose in each, and then flying to the arms of the other. All the energy that goes into the work, the force of imagination and concentration, *is* a kind of autobiographical energy, no matter what one is actually writing about. One has to give to one's work like a lover. One must give of oneself, and try not to pick fights. Perhaps it *is* something of a sickness – halfway between 'quarantine and operetta' (to steal a phrase from Celine) – to write intensely, closely – not with one's pen at arm's length, but perhaps with one's arm out of the way entirely, one's hand up under one's arm, near the heart, thrashing out like a flipper, one's face hovering close above the page, listening with ear and cheek, lips forming the words. Martha Graham speaks of the Icelandic term 'doom eager' to denote that ordeal of isolation, restlessness, caughtness an artist experiences when he or she is sick with an idea.

When a writer is doom eager, the writing won't be sludge on the page; it will give readers – and the writer, of course, is the very first reader – an experience they've never had before, or perhaps a little and at last the words for an experience they have. The writing will disclose a world; it will be that Heideggerean 'setting-itself-into-work of the truth of what is'. But it will not have lost the detail; detail, on its own, contains the universe. As Eudora Welty said, 'It's always necessary to remember that the fiction writer is much less immediately concerned with grand ideas than he is with putting list slippers on clerks.' One must think of the craft – that impulse to make an object from the materials lying about, as much as of the spiritual longing, the philosophical sweep. 'It is impossible to experience one's own death objectively,' Woody Allen once said, 'and still carry a tune.'

Obviously one must keep a certain amount of literary faith, and not be afraid to travel with one's work into margins and jungles and danger zones, and one should also live with someone who can cook and who will both be with one and leave one alone. But there is no formula, to the life or to the work, and all any writer

finally knows are the little decisions he or she has been forced to make, given the particular choices. There's no golden recipe. Most things literary are stubborn as colds; they resist all formulas – a chemist's, a wet nurse's, a magician's. Finally, there is no formula outside the sick devotion to the work. Perhaps one would be wise when young even to avoid thinking of oneself as a writer – for there's something a little stopped and satisfied, too healthy, in that. Better to think of *writing*, of what one does as an activity, rather than an identity – to write, I write; we write; to keep the calling a verb rather than a noun; to keep working at the thing, at all hours, in all places, so that your life does not become a pose, a pornography of wishing. William Carlos Williams said, 'Catch an eyeful, catch an earful, and don't drop what you've caught.' He was a doctor. So presumably he knew about *sicker* and *better* and how they are often quite close.

MY WATERLOO

Josephine Hart

[My novels] were conceived as I raced around London, head down, lost in imaginary conversations with myself, and indeed sometimes so overcome with emotion that I would find myself weeping in the street.

Josephine Hart was a magazine publisher and drama producer before writing her first novel, *Damage*, in six weeks. It
became an international best-seller and has been filmed by
Louis Malle. She has since published a second novel, *Sin*,
which was short-listed for the *Sunday Express* Award.

MY WATERLOO

For most of my adult life I resisted writing.

I fought an 'internal battle' with the words, characters and lives that inhabited my mind, and at times threatened to devour it. I superimposed on this assault of the imagination, initially – and most strangely – a business career in magazine publishing, then a career as a theatre producer – accompanied by a short sortie into television.

I was married to a man who had witnessed my struggles for many years – first as a friend, later as a husband. He was determined that I would lose and that my imagination would win. He contrived with a mixture of patience and cunning to bring about my Waterloo.

In the summer of 1989 I finally collapsed on to the page. As though insane with relief, the words poured from their prison.

The cause of my long terror of writing lies deeper than I care to go. Since *Damage* was written in the first person of a male character, and set in a world different from my own, the root cause was clearly not a fear of autobiography. Perhaps I knew my writing came from the 'edge of things', and I recognized it to be dangerous. However, with *Damage* I took an irreversible step. Like its main character, there was no going back for me either.

Damage had been completed in my head long before I sat down to write it – as indeed was my new novel *Sin* and four other yet-to-be 'freed' novels. They were conceived and nurtured as I raced around London, head down, lost in imaginary conversations with my characters, and indeed sometimes so overcome by their emotions that I would find myself weeping in the street.

Flaubert said: 'We do not choose our subjects. They choose us.' That is the most succinct explanation of the mystery of where characters came from and why they want their story told. Through the years of 'repression' the voice of the main character in *Damage* remained powerful. I became more and more connected to his conscience. And as I traced my way through its labyrinthine path, his emotional, psychological and sexual strengths and weaknesses became increasingly clear to me. The other people, who had helped to form him and his view of life, slowly crystallized. Stendhal speaks of the discovery of love as a process of 'crystallization'. It is, I believe, a perfect description of the process through which characters move into focus.

So where did I – the author – come in? Firstly, in finding the precise voice in which my character could tell his story. A voice, which through the rhythms and textures of its language, would comment on the tale being told. Secondly, in the organization of his world and time towards the climactic moment when the consequences of his tragic flaw – what Aristotle calls *hamartia* – are revealed. Thirdly, in the search for a philosophical truth which would lead to catharsis, both for the character and for the reader.

My own obsessions no doubt played their part, hidden beneath the structure of the book. Though fiercely controlled by me, they occasionally escaped: my intellectual obsession with the psychology of sex – how it determines the choreography of desire. And my long private dialogue with death and its aftermath. All of this was known and understood by me before I put my pen to paper.

I wrote *Damage* in six weeks during a summer holiday in France. I wrote for a maximum of three hours each morning, in illegible longhand, in a child's copy book. I always stopped at 12.30 irrespective of how I felt the writing was progressing. Whenever a wave of intense creativity threatened to break over me, I got up and walked away. I refused to 'go with it'. That, I believe, gave *Damage* the 'controlled intensity' I felt essential to the story.

My secretary of sixteen years – the only person who could decipher my writing – started to type the manuscript. I then undertook that exquisitely painful pursuit of perfection known as editing. This was physically exhausting – from early morning until late in the evening – intellectually exhilarating, and as Dame Iris Murdoch said it would be, finally, 'addictive'.

Later I spent a month reading *Damage* out loud to myself over and over again. Looking for the rhythm of the language. Because I had always been an Eliot fanatic I had produced a number of poetry events in London celebrating his work. One particular production taught me a fascinating lesson concerning the hypnotic power of the hidden beat in language. The first half of the evening comprised *The Waste Land*, 'Portrait of a Lady' and 'The Hollow Men'. *Four Quartets* – an hour-long poem – was presented in the second half. Not normal West End fare! Yet the second half, with its enormous intellectual demands, was a triumph. As though in a trance the audience followed the actors, Eileen Atkins, Edward Fox and Michael Gough, through that extraordinary journey of the soul. The strange rhythm and beat of the words – their meaning not always clear to everyone – created a magical world from which it was impossible to escape.

That is my ambition when writing. To make it impossible for the reader to escape. In *Damage* words were changed and sentences restructured in this cause. I was not trying for 'street credibility' or for an exact re-creation of reality, but to unlock the truth that hides behind reality, using language as the key.

I have since finished my second book, *Sin*. The pattern was the same. It's the way I write. It's the only way I can.

A TRY FOR GREATNESS
Robertson Davies

The way of telling the tale may and must change, but is the tale really a new one? If the writer thinks of himself not as a successor to the Georgians, but as one of the line of Aesop and Scheherazade and the tirelessly inventive author of *The Golden Legend*, he need not worry too much about the latest literary fashions from the Parisian literary couturiers.

Robertson Davies is Master Emeritus and Professor Emeritus at the University of Toronto, Canada. A playwright, novelist, critic and actor, his 1986 novel, *What's Bred in the Bone* (part of *The Cornish Trilogy*), was nominated for the Booker Prize. His most recent novel is *Murther & Walking Spirits*.

A TRY FOR GREATNESS

SINCE 1945 there has been observable a tendency to use the term Man of Letters in real or implied quotation marks, as though speaking of a vanishing or vanished species. An admirable book, *The Rise and Fall of the Man of Letters*, by John Gross (1969) seems by its title to suggest an obituary of the breed, but that is to misunderstand it; the writer's conclusion is that 'the idea of the man of letters has a place in any healthy literary tradition'. It seems to me that the Man of Letters is still with us and must be seen in modern terms. What is the Man of Letters? There is no mystery about it; he is a writer, perhaps a poet or a novelist, who also turns his hand, when he chooses, to criticism, reviewing, essays, controversy, journalism or anything else that may engage the attention of one whose principal concern is with literature and the arts; he is a man who makes his reputation and his living by the pen, and has gained some acceptance by doing so.

We do not have to look far for modern examples of the Man of Letters. Sir Victor Pritchett is, surely, at the top of the list and the names of many writers of fiction and verse, of biography and comment follow naturally. Consider the contributors to this book; men and women of letters one and all, and they are but a few of those now living. Requiems for the Man of Letters are foolishly premature and are attempted only by those who fear their level gaze.

During the past quarter century or so, however, the range of the Man of Letters has been extended in a direction that is new, and perhaps dangerous. We are now familiar with the Man of Letters as Travelling Showman. Every spring and autumn we are

aware of scores and very likely hundreds of authors of all kinds who are jaunting from town to town reading from their work, appearing on radio and television shows, signing books in shops, and being interviewed by the press. Whenever a writer of established reputation brings out a new book he is expected to hit the trail, and if he is a new author of promise, he is dangled before possible readers as a desirable *parti*, not to be overlooked by those who want to be in the literary swim. Like Shakespeare before him, he may say . . . *I have gone here and there And made myself a motley to the view*.

It is the publishers who arrange these jaunts. They assure the author that there is no publicity like it and, although it is in his power to refuse to travel, by so doing he is biting off his nose to spite his face. Never before has the reading public had such an appetite for watching the author as he writes his name over and over again on the title page of his book, smiling as warmly as he may on the many who assure him that they are 'his greatest fan'. And somewhat excitable as such declarations are, there is no reason to doubt the sincerity of their feeling.

The author reads from his work. This is a chancy business, for he may not be a good reader; he may loathe the idea of public performance; he may simply have no notion of how to make his reading acceptable as a pleasurable experience. Some of the finest writers are bad readers, as anybody who has listened to recordings of the reading of T. S. Eliot or Robert Graves can attest; in dull, strangulated voices, the poets offer their treasures. A notable exception was Dylan Thomas, and there were malcontents who said that his works were lesser poetry on the page than when he declaimed them; to which it must be replied that declamation is vastly older than silent reading, and a bard may reasonably be expected to declaim like a bard. For the best of reasons I offer no living examples. Authors have told me that they think it degrading to read their work aloud and they only do it under compulsion. (And for the money, of course; as Tyrone Guthrie used to say, when confronted with this sort of wincing pudency, 'We artists

despise money, but of course we like to have a little to buy flowers.') There are authors like myself who think that to agree to read, and then to read ineptly or badly, is simply to take money under false pretences; a bard, even a prose bard, must raise the spirits and charm the ear.

The reading is only a part of the work of the travelling author; he must be interviewed. If the interviewer is a skilled hand, the interview becomes an agreeable conversation. But such interviewers – informed, friendly, acquainted with the author's work – are not met with everywhere, and too often the interview becomes an hour-long interrogation, sinking to unanswerable queries such as, 'Where do you get your ideas from?' (*If I knew, do you suppose I'd tell you?*) and 'What's your work schedule?' (*I drink a bottle of brandy at midnight, coax my raven on to the pallid bust of Pallas above my chamber door, and scribble till dawn*). The interrogation of a bad interviewer is comparable to that of the secret police, and the author grows restless and then weary as it goes on for a long afternoon in a hotel bedroom. A time comes when he will say anything, admit to anything, to bring the questioning to an end. And then, of course, there is the added terror of the photographer who comes with the pressman. An author must be vain indeed if he does not dread their ceaseless scrutiny.

The author does it for money. If a reading or an autographing sells more books he will do it because that is how he gets his living. There is nothing ignominious about it, though it is an exploitation of personality that has little to do with the quality of the book that is being touted. And publishers make such tours flattering to writers whose home life may not be luxurious. The successful author is carried from place to place on a silver tray; air tickets and private cars are provided; he stays at good hotels and may eat and drink himself into a stupor if he is silly enough to do it. Agreeable women from the publisher's staff shepherd him from place to place, and protect him from the nuisances who want him to read typescripts of unpublished work, or be photographed with a cherished infant, or simply to listen to their torrent of talk, as

his senses reel. The promotion tour, as it is called, is hard work, but it is flattering and who is averse to a little flattery, provided it is cloaked in a deceptive delicacy?

But does this role of the Travelling Showman leave his work as an author untouched? Hard work as the job of the Travelling Showman is, it has obvious extrovert compensations that the solitary work of the author lacks.

Much depends on how the author regards himself and his work. If the greatest possible degree of popular appeal, and the sales bought by such appeal, are what he aims at, he will gladly undertake his task as Travelling Showman. At a recent book fair in Gothenburg I saw Miss Jackie Collins besieged by fans, many of whom obviously read her work, and all of whom were wild to have a look at her; she was the undoubted Queen of the Fair. When some of the children who could not get near their goddess applied to me for an autograph, and I signed it 'Jackie Collins' they ran away delighted, if a little puzzled. But many authors want recognition, if they can get it, only for their best work. They take themselves, as authors, with a seriousness that does not tip the balance toward the Travelling Showman. And though they may do their promotion tours honestly, they sicken in their hearts of what Hazlitt called 'the nuisance of importunate, tormenting, everlasting personal identity'. He knew what it was like, for he got a part of his living as a lecturer, and was of such quality that Keats once walked seven miles to hear him speak.

So – how does the modern writer see himself? Does he ever, I wonder, think of himself in terms of what Carlyle says in his essay 'The Hero as Man of Letters': 'The Man of Letters is sent hither specially that he may discern for himself, and make manifest to us, this same Divine Idea; in every generation it will manifest itself in a new dialect; and he is here for the supreme purpose of doing that . . . Fichte speaks of the Unspeakable Divine Significance full of splendour, of wonder and terror, that lies in the being of every man, of every thing – the Presence of the God who made every man and thing.' This is asking for a very great deal and asking for

it with Carlyle's unsparing seriousness of language and thought. But is it asking too much of the committed literary artist? Is it really asking more than Cyril Connolly asks for when he says that the one function of a writer is to produce a masterpiece and no other task is of any consequence? Is it more rigorous than the demands of F. R. Leavis? It calls on the writer to make a try for greatness, and not to fail for lack of serious commitment.

Nor is Carlyle's demand as alarming as it seems. When he tells us that his three nominations for heroism in Men of Letters are Samuel Johnson, Rousseau and Robert Burns, we breathe more freely, for surely no stranger trio was ever brought together under one label.

The spirit of our time does not encourage writers, or indeed anyone else, to think of themselves in terms of greatness. Perhaps the last writer who would have gravely accepted that word as applied to himself was Thomas Mann, and his acceptance would not have been simple vanity; he regarded himself as the upholder of the tradition of Goethe, and he had reason to believe that several hundred thousand readers agreed with him. But what tradition does the present-day writer in English think of himself as continuing? Indeed, any conscious harking-back is sharply rebuked by the reviewers, and the academic critics who are so busy devising new bottles for the old, old wine that any reminders of a literary tradition are repugnant to them.

The old, old wine – is it not that which the writer seeks to renew and rival with the grapes from his own vineyard? Has the life of man, the human spirit and the turn of Fortune's wheel changed so irrevocably during the past five hundred years that we who write today have no kinship and no descent from those who wrote yesterday and many yesterdays ago? The way of telling the tale may and must change, but is the tale really a new one? If the writer thinks of himself not as a successor to the Georgians, but as one of the line of Aesop and Scheherazade and the tirelessly inventive author of *The Golden Legend*, he need not worry too much about the latest literary fashions from the Parisian literary couturiers.

The terrible truth will out. Everybody knows it, but at present it is thought better not to be too explicit about it. Nevertheless it must be said: every writer is, in one way or another, a moralist. Not, let me hasten to say, that he seeks to impose ideas of truth and conduct on his readers – though the more innocent writers of sensation novels, and especially writers of crime fiction, do so without any objection being raised – but because he observes life from the standpoint of his own spirit and personality, and he records what he sees: certain courses of action bring, inevitably, certain consequences.

> That the Dog returns to his vomit,
> and the Sow returns to her mire,
> And the burnt Fool's bandaged finger
> goes wabbling back to the Fire . . .

He may be a genius without illusion, like Shakespeare, or a world-saver, like Tolstoy, or a philosopher and ironist, like Thomas Mann, or an agonist, like Dostoevsky, or an illuminator of dark corners, like Dickens, but he tells us what he sees the way he sees it; in the infinite variety of tales told, or wisdom distilled in poetry, an astonishingly small number of essential truths emerge. It is in the depth of his understanding of these, rather than in any remarkable breadth, that whatever of greatness resides within him will show itself.

That, as Bully Bottom says, will require some tears in the true performance of it. To be a writer, striving to write as best he can, is not a jolly, high-hearted occupation. Indeed it is lonely work and the introspection it demands is fatiguing to body and mind. The writer may growl at Carlyle's notion of the Hero as Man of Letters, but can he escape the demand that he seek for that which is full of splendour and wonder and terror, even if he chokes on the Unspeakable Divine Significance Fichte declares to be its origin? Fichte was no fool.

Heroism in the literary world is by no means unknown in our time. To name but one among many who have dared greatly,

ROBERTSON DAVIES

Miss Nadine Gordimer has taken serious risks and endured much obloquy to say what she knows must be said. The Man of Letters as Hero is no stranger in our time, but the recognition of heroes is as reluctant as it has ever been. The heroism of Miss Gordimer and those who, like her, have demanded recognition for the splendour, the wonder and the terror which Fichte calls the Presence of God in every man and thing, rebukes the Travelling Showman side of authorship and calls us back to our greater purpose.

If the writer is so happy as to have a protean streak in his nature, he may encompass the Travelling Showman as well, taking care that the Travelling Showman, with his drum and trumpet, does not drown out and eventually silence the other and finer voice. But the temptation is great and constant vigilance is needed to escape the wiles of the tempter.

THREE IN A BED:
FICTION, MORALS AND POLITICS

Nadine Gordimer

Not every fiction writer entering a relation with politics trades imagination for the hair shirt of the party hack.

Vivid and outspoken author of many novels and short stories set in her native South Africa, Nadine Gordimer's books include *Burger's Daughter*, *July's People* and *My Son's Story*. She was a joint winner of the Booker Prize with her novel, *The Conservationist*. She has won many other literary prizes and in 1991 was awarded the Nobel Prize for Literature. Her most recent publication is the short-story collection, *Why Haven't You Written?*

THREE IN A BED:
FICTION, MORALS AND POLITICS

Three in a bed: it's a kinky cultural affair. I had better identify the partners.

Politics and morals, as concepts, need no introduction, although their relationship is shadily ambiguous. But fiction has defining responsibilities I shall be questioning, so I shall begin right away with the basic, dictionary definition of what fiction is supposed to be.

Fiction, says the Oxford English Dictionary, is 'the action of feigning or inventing imaginary existences, events, states of things'. Fiction, collectively, is prose novels and stories. So poetry, according to the OED, is not fiction. The more I ponder this, the more it amazes me; the more I challenge it. Does the poet not invent imaginary existences, events, states of things?

Now what is politics doing in bed with fiction? Morals have bedded with story-telling since the magic of the imaginative capacity developed in the human brain – and in my ignorance of a scientific explanation of changes in the cerebrum or whatever, to account for this faculty, I believe it was the inkling development that here was somewhere where the truth about being alive might lie. The harsh lessons of daily existence, co-existence between human and human, with animals and nature, could be made sense of in the ordering of properties of the transforming imagination, working on the 'states of things'. With this faculty fully developed, great art in fiction can evolve in imaginative revelation to fit the crises of an age that comes after its own, undreamt of when it was written. *Moby Dick* can now be seen as an allegory of

environmental tragedy. 'The whale is the agent of cosmic retribution':* we have sought to destroy the splendid creature that is nature, believing we could survive only by 'winning' a battle against nature; now we see our death in the death of nature, brought about by ourselves.

Morals are the husband/wife of fiction. And politics? Politics somehow followed morals in, picking the lock and immobilizing the alarm system. At first it was in the dark, perhaps, and fiction thought the embrace of politics was that of morals, didn't know the difference . . . And this is understandable. Morals and politics have a family connection. Politics' ancestry is morality – way back, and generally accepted as forgotten. The resemblance is faded. In the light of morning, if fiction accepts the third presence within the sheets it is soon in full cognizance of who and what politics is.

The relationship of fiction with politics has not had the kind of husbandly/fatherly authoritarian sanction that morals, with their religious origins, lingeringly has. No literary critic I know of suggests that *moralizing* as opposed to 'immorality' has no place in fiction, whereas many works of fiction are declared 'spoiled' by the writer's recognition of politics as a motivation of character as great as sex or religion. Of course, this lack of sanction is characteristic of an affair, a wild affair in which great tensions arise, embraces and repulsions succeed one another, distress and celebration are confused, loyalty and betrayal change place, accusations fly. And whether the fiction writer gets involved with politics initially through his/her convictions as a citizen pushing within against the necessary detachment of the writer, or whether by the pressure of seduction from without, the same problems in the relationship arise and have to be dealt with *in the fiction* as well as in the life.

For when have writers not lived in times of political conflict? Whose Golden Age, whose *belle époque*, whose Roaring Twenties

* '. . . to Ahab, the whale is the agent of cosmic retribution.' Harry Levin, 'The Jonah Complex', from *The Power of Blackness*, p. 215, Vintage Books, 1960.

were these so-named lovely times? The time of slave and peasant misery, while sculptors sought perfect proportions of the human torso? The time of revolutionaries in Czar Alexander's prisons, while Grand Dukes built mansions in Nice? The time of the hungry and unemployed offered the salvation of growing Fascism, while playboys and girls danced balancing glasses of pink champagne?

When, overtly or implicitly, could writers evade politics? Even those writers who have seen fiction as the pure exploration of language, as music is the exploration of sound – the babbling of Dada and the page-shuffling attempts of Burroughs have been in reaction to what each revolted against in the politically imposed spirit of their respective times; literary movements which were an act – however far-out – of acknowledgement of a relationship between politics and fiction.

It seems there is no getting away from the relationship. On the one hand, we live in what Seamus Heaney* calls a world where the 'undirected play of the imagination is regarded at best as luxury or licentiousness, at worst as heresy or treason. In ideal republics ... it is a common expectation that the writer will sign over his or her venturesome and potentially disruptive activity into the keeping of official doctrine, traditional system, a party line, whatever ...'

We are shocked by such clear cases of creativity outlawed. But things are not always so drastically simple. Not every fiction writer entering a relation with politics trades imagination for the hair shirt of the party hack. There is also the case of the writer whose imaginative powers are genuinely roused by and involved with the spirit of politics as she or he personally experiences it. This may be virtually inescapable in times and places of socially seismic upheaval. Society shakes, the walls of entities fall; the writer has known the evil, indifference or cupidity of the old order, and the spirit of creativity naturally pushes towards new

---

* Seamus Heaney, *The Government of the Tongue*, p. 96, Faber and Faber, 1988.

growth. The writer is moved to fashion an expression of a new order, accepted on trust as an advance in human freedom that therefore also will be the release of a greater creativity.

'Russia became a garden of nightingales. Poets sprang up as never before. People barely had the strength to live but they were all singing' – so wrote Andrey Bely in the early days of the Russian revolution. One of Pasternak's latest biographers, Peter Levi,* notes that Pasternak – popularly known to the West on the evidence of his disillusioned *Dr Zhivago* as *the* anti-Communist writer – in his young days contributed manifestos to the 'infighting of the day'. In his poem to Stalin† he sang:

> We want the glorious. We want the good.
> We want to see things free from fear.
> Unlike some fancy fop, the spendthrift
> of his bright, brief span, we yearn
> for labour shared by everyone,
> for the common discipline of law.

This yearning is addressed by writers in different ways, as fiction seeks a proper relation with politics. In the Soviet Union of Pasternak's day, some fell into what the Italian contemporary writer, Claudio Magris,‡ in a different context, calls with devastating cynicism 'A sincere but perverted passion for freedom, which led . . . into mechanical servitude, as is the way with sin'. The noble passion deteriorated to the tragically shabby, as in the 1930s the Writers' Union turned on itself to beat out all but mediocrity mouthing platitudes, driving Mayakovsky to suicide and turning down Pasternak's plea to be granted a place where he would have somewhere other than a freezing partitioned slice of a room in which to write and live. Yet Pasternak had not abandoned belief –

* Peter Levi, *Boris Pasternak*, p. 77, Hutchinson, 1990.
† Boris Pasternak, quoted by Evgeny Pasternak in *Boris Pasternak, The Tragic Years 1930–60*, p. 38, Collins Harvill, 1990.
‡ Claudio Magris, *Inferences on a Sabre*, translated from the Italian by Mark Thompson, p. 43, Polygon, 1990.

never did – in the original noble purpose of revolution, although for him the writing of this period became, by the edicts of the State and the Writers' Union, 'a train derailed and lying at the bottom of an embankment'.

Politics is not always the murderer of fiction. The Brechts and Nerudas survive, keeping the revolutionary vision. But the relation, like all vital ones, always implies some danger. The first dismaying discovery for the writer is once again best expressed by Magris's* cynicism: 'the lie is quite as real as the truth, it works upon the world, transforms it'; whereas the fiction writer, in pursuit of truth beyond the guise of reasoning, has believed that truth, however elusive, is the only reality. Yet we have seen the lie transforming; we have had Goebbels. And his international descendants, practising that transformation on the people of a number of countries, including the white people of my own country, who accepted the lie that apartheid was both divinely decreed and secularly just, and created a society on it.

To be aware that the lie also can transform the world places an enormous responsibility on art to counter this with its own transformations. The *knowledge* that the writer's searching and intuition gain instinctively contradicts the lie.

> We page through each other's faces
> we read each looking eye . . .
> It has taken lives to be able to do so

writes the South African poet, Mongane Wally Serote.† We may refuse to write according to any orthodoxy, we may refuse to toe any party line, even that drawn by the cause we know to be just, and our own, but we cannot refuse the responsibility of what we know. What we know beyond surface reality has to become

* Ibid. p. 63.
† Mongane Wally Serote, *A Tough Tale*, p. 7, Kliptown Books, 1987.

what, again in Serote's words, 'We want the world to know'; we must in this, our inescapable relation with politics, 'page for wisdom through the stubborn night'.

THE ARTIST AND INTEGRITY

Amos Oz

... the writer ... is equipped to act as the language's smoke
detector, if not its fire brigade ... he can use his words for
building castles, for playing brilliant games, for calling death
a rose. But he is also capable, and therefore responsible, for
calling a rose a rose, and a lie a lie.

Amos Oz – acclaimed as Israel's finest living writer – is the author of seven novels, including the celebrated *My Michael*, and an assessment of his native country, *In the Land of Israel*. His most recent work is *Unto Death: Two Stories*.

THE ARTIST AND INTEGRITY

There is no Hebrew word for integrity: perhaps we Jews lack this 'Roman' quality altogether. In my dictionary I found, among other synonyms for integrity, 'intactness, wholeness, being firm, in one piece'. We Jews are probably made of several pieces, not of one.

Can we really expect a poet or a story-teller to be 'whole' or 'intact' in any sense? Can the inventor of plots and characters, the creator of a substitute reality, be 'firm, in one piece'? Isn't he or she forever in the business of shuttering and piecing together? Isn't the poet or the writer dealing with mosaic rather than with a block of marble? Fascinated by the differential rather than the integral of things?

D.H. Lawrence once said that a story-teller must be capable of presenting several conflicting and contradictory points of view with an equal degree of conviction. Just like that rabbi in the old Jewish story, the one who decreed that both rival claims over a goat were right, and later on, at home, when asked by his son how both could be right, replied with a sigh, 'And you too, my son, are right.'

Poets and story-tellers are sometimes regarded as witnesses. One tends to expect a certain integrity from a witness, at least integrity in the sense of honesty, sincerity and objectivity. Writers usually testify for the prosecution yet they are also witnesses for the defence. Worse still: the poet is a member of the jury. Yet isn't he also the interrogator who has exposed, unmasked the accused? And isn't he or she, at the same time, a relative of the accused? And the family of the victim, too? He or she may act as the judge

as well. He may secretly plot an escape while arming the jailer. Can such a dubious character have any integrity at all?

But let's consider the role of the writer as a defender of the language: the one who is equipped to act as the language's smoke detector, if not its fire brigade.

Tyranny, oppression, moral degeneration, persecution and mass killing have always and everywhere started with the pollution of the language, with making it sound clean and decent where it should have been base and violent ('the new order', 'final solution', 'temporary measures', 'limited restrictions') or else with making the language sound coarse and bestial where it should have been humane and delicate ('parasites', 'social insects', 'political cancer', etc.). I said the writer ought to be a smoke detector, if not a fire brigade, within his or her own language because wherever a human being is referred to as a parasite or a germ, there follow, sooner or later, death squads and exterminations. Wherever war is called peace, where oppression and persecution are referred to as security, and assassination is called liberation, the defilement of the language precedes and prepares the defilement of life and dignity. In the end, the state, the regime, the class or the idea remain intact where human life is shattered. Integrity prevails over the fields of scattered bodies.

My own excursions into political essays started with a 'linguistic reservation'. In 1967, immediately after the Six Day War (which I regarded as a right battle for Israel's self-defence) I wrote an article objecting to the use of the term 'liberated territories'. I insisted that territories simply cannot be liberated, that the term 'liberation' can only refer to people, not to vales and mountains. Fifteen years later, writing about the Israeli invasion into Lebanon in 1982 (to which I fiercely objected) I wrote an essay stating my bewilderment at the official Israeli title for that bloody war: 'Operation Peace for Galilee'. A war, I argued, even the most justifiable one, cannot be called peace.

Back to our dubious character whose integrity begins and ends

within the domain of words: he can use his words for building castles, for playing brilliant games, for calling death a rose. But he is also capable, and therefore responsible, for calling a rose a rose, and a lie a lie, for calling villainy villainy, and torture torture. His way of screaming 'fire' makes him the horror of tyrants. Isn't every censorship in the world an indirect manifestation of awe and admiration for the power of the writer's words? We are talking about tyrants who usually have their lunatic integrity but who are terrified of those wordly characters who lack integrity. They are afraid of the writer because he knows them intimately, he knows them through and through – he has journeyed through their minds. Nothing is alien to this dubious character. Every madness, savagery, obscenity and ruthlessness in the mind of the tyrant must have crossed the poet's mind as well.

I doubt if writers and poets have integrity or even should have. I think though that some of us are capable of defusing the deadly integrity of the fanatic, the monomaniac, the raging ideologist, the murderous crusader. I think fanaticism is 'their' department, whereas comparative fanaticism is ours. Let them dwell in their marble monuments – we dwell in our patient and precise mosaics.

PLOT LUCK

John Mortimer

... the hours spent writing are like giving a performance on the page ... This is why writing fiction is exhausting; it's not the mechanical process that tires you out but the stage fright, the tension and the final collapse in the dressing room and the first drink of the evening.

John Mortimer is a barrister, dramatist and novelist whose Rumpole stories and novels – mainly wry studies of the English abroad – are hugely popular. His latest novel is *Dunster*.

PLOT LUCK

I was sitting beside a pool in Morocco and in front of me there was a party of chartered accountants, spread out in a row of beds, no doubt out there for some conference or annual jaunt. One of them, we'll call him Ted, said, 'What are you reading, Mike?' and Mike admitted that it was a novel. 'Isn't that fiction?' Ted sounded disgusted. 'I don't see any point in that stuff. I mean, if it's not true why bother to read it?'

To which Mike replied with great good sense, 'You could say exactly the same thing about accounts.'

Why bother to write fiction? There are so many answers and every writer will give you a different one. To earn a crust? To satisfy our basic instinct, since we lived in caves and hunted mammoths, to tell stories and enjoy the fact that people gather round to listen? To make some sort of order out of a chaotic universe, or to expel some old devils from inside us and send them out into the world? Whatever our motives one thing is certain: our work can't be any good unless we tell the truth about life as we see it. Mike was right. Balance sheets are the work of creative artists. Politicians, it goes without saying, live almost entirely in a world of fiction, usually of a rather tedious variety. Lawyers frequently manage to obscure the truth and judges very seldom discover it. When I practised the law I used to leave the Old Bailey, the world of fantasy and make believe, where everyone wore fancy dress and behaved like judges and barristers and criminals in very old British movies which they'd seen long ago, and go down to some draughty rehearsal room where a collection

of actors and actresses, rehearsing a fictional play, were at least trying to say something truthful about our existence. A villain on trial may lie and get away with it; if a novelist doesn't mean what he says he's condemned forever.

None of this means that a novel should tell the truth in the way of a news item or a documentary film; indeed nothing can lie more effectively than a piece of 'straight' reporting. It must arrive at its conclusions, or at least ask its questions, through the working of the imagination, the telling of stories and the creation of characters. The novelist has a duty which he must perform before he starts illuminating the human condition. He must entertain the audience. Matisse, perhaps the greatest painter of this century, said somewhere that people lead difficult lives, they work hard and they are beset with anxiety at the end of the day. It is the first task of the artist, said Matisse, to make them feel relaxed, to entertain them and to give them pleasure. This essential function of the artist is one, so it seems to me, that is inclined to be forgotten today. For this reason the hours spent writing are like giving a performance on the page, a prolonged one-man show which will grip the audience's attention and keep the customers laughing or crying or being alarmed or continually wondering what's going to happen next. This is why writing fiction is exhausting; it's not the mechanical process that tires you out but the stage fright, the tension and the final collapse in the dressing room and the first drink of the evening.

Just as an audience in the theatre must be kept watching, as their attention must be held so that they don't walk out, or indulge in a fit of terminal bronchitis, or rustle chocolate wrapping papers, so the novel reader must be induced to sit still and go on turning the pages.

And something else of great importance seems to have gone out of style. The word 'plot' has almost become a term of abuse, and yet unless the book tells a story the reader won't be induced to turn the pages. The story may be a magnificent one, as in *Great Expectations* or *Treasure Island* or *The Wings Of A Dove*. It may

be, as is the plot of *Bleak House*, complex and somewhat obscure, so if you were challenged you might be hard put to remember it. What you remember are Harold Skimpole and Grandpa Smallweed and the great elegy for Jo the crossing sweeper, the marvellous comic or sinister set pieces which are strung along the plot like fireworks on a wire. But if there were no story you wouldn't go on reading and the book's pleasures would be missed forever.

Plots are essential, but plots are the hardest part; at any rate I find this to be so. Everything else about writing can be done by turning up regularly on the empty page and starting the performance. Plots are notoriously shy and retiring. With luck they may visit you in unexpected places, in the bath or while waiting in the doctor's surgery. Very often they stay away altogether and are always out in a meeting and don't return your call. Then it's no good sitting and waiting for them, you have to start writing, you have to begin to create characters. And then, as a character begins to talk, or comes into conflict with another, the plot may start working; because it's important that the characters perform the plot and the plot doesn't manipulate the characters. This process is a mysterious one and the most exciting part of writing fiction. Most novelists have experienced the magical moment when a character has come so completely to life that he or she will do something quite unexpected, something the author had never intended and which sends the story off into new and uncharted territory. The moment when the characters take charge is one of great happiness for the writer; it must be hoped for but cannot be planned and is only rarely foreseen. For this reason it's not worth, in my experience, making elaborate notes of a story before you start it – with any luck you might be able to write a short synopsis when past three-quarters of the way through. Still less is it worth doing elaborate research, research is best done after the book is finished. The only thing to do is to sit down and start, for plots are more often attracted by the clatter of the typewriter, or the scratch of the pen across an empty page.

I was encouraged in this way of going to work by reading

about Georges Feydeau, the great writer of French farces, whose plots are as intricate and precisely fashioned as the inside of a gold watch. Surely his plays had to be meticulously planned? Not at all. It seems that the eccentric Feydeau sat down in his bedroom near the Gare du Nord (he booked in there for a weekend whilst his wife was moving house and stayed for the rest of his life) and started to write with no idea of what was going to happen on the next page. But soon he began to create such tempting characters and situations that plots came rushing to his aid.

So writing a novel is not only a performance. It's like flying blind, with few instruments and no map, towards some vaguely imagined destination. It's the invention of stories which will entertain and, with any luck, tell some sort of truth. Of course it may not be literal truth, it may be legendary and imaginative truth, but it should have some significant relation to the world we live in.

Sometimes the legends are taken as fact. A few years ago I decided to write a 'Rumpole' story about a court martial. I had never participated in this sort of military tribunal, so I went off to the British Army in Germany and watched a soldier being tried for allegedly smoking a cannabis cigarette. The only evidence of the nature of the cigarette was that he had said it contained dope, and it was suggested that he might have been boasting or telling a lie.

Having discovered as much as I could about the court-martial procedure I came back to England and wrote a story called 'Rumpole and the Bright Seraphim'. In this entirely fictional work a British Army sergeant is found stabbed through the heart, wearing a woman's scarlet evening dress, outside a discothèque in Germany. A private soldier is court-martialled for the murder. This story was published and filmed for television.

Some two years later I was invited to visit the Guards in West Germany. Before dinner I had a drink in the Sergeants' Mess, and I was asked if I had visited the Army in Germany before. I said I had and that I'd gone to see a rather interesting trial of a young

soldier who'd said he was smoking a cannabis cigarette. 'Oh no you didn't,' one of them said. 'You were over here about that case we had where a sergeant was found stabbed through the heart wearing a woman's scarlet evening dress outside a disco.' I had a curious feeling of elation, almost as great as that which comes when one of your characters takes over the plot. Fiction had become real life, and it was a very curious moment indeed.

WRITERS AT WORK

What are the ideal conditions for creative writing – or do they exist only in fiction? Four eminent authors tell a strange tale of getting to grips with life's obstacles and employing them as part of the curious structure that is a writer's life.

These articles originally appeared in the *Guardian* as part of a series of interviews by Clare Boylan.

Anthony Burgess

'I work at a large architect's table in a chalet-type house in Lugano which is so new that it has an air raid shelter. The door of this is so heavy that my wife and I together cannot open it, but occasionally we manage and it is used for storing copies of *Corriere della Sera*, a Milanese paper to which I contribute.'

Burgess is homesick for his room with a view in an old building on the Rue Grimaldi in Monte Carlo. 'But it is on the third floor and with my bad heart and my wife's bad leg we cannot manage the stairs. We have been trying to have a lift put in for the past twelve years, but the matter is still under discussion.'

He has a word processor for journalism but writes fiction directly on to a typewriter. 'It is a very old manual – by far the best. Electric typewriters keep going "mmmmmmm – what are you waiting for?" So does the word processor. I never use a notebook but I waste a very great deal of paper as I am endlessly re-writing. I'm afraid there will be no manuscripts for the university archives. What I have done in the making of a book is nobody's business. The rest is just waste paper.

'Of course one never gets it right. The poet Valéry once said, "You don't finish a poem – you abandon it." It is the same with a novel. You don't say, "I've done it!" You come, with a kind of horrible desperation, to realize that this will do.'

Burgess was only ever completely happy with one of his works. 'It was a novel written in the seventies, called *MF*. I worked very hard on it and it was flung into a great silence. It was a structuralist work relating to the literary association between incest and the riddle. The title related to the hero's name, Miles Farmer. It also

referred to male and female and to the inspiration for the work, which was a remark by the American actor William Conrad who once said to me: "It's time someone wrote an updated version of Oedipus, called Motherfucker."'

Anthony Burgess writes from nine to five and endeavours to produce three pages of finished copy every day. 'I have no distractions when I'm working. I don't eat or drink anything. As I get older I find I am not interested in food. Sometimes I eat a bar of chocolate because I am told there is iron in it. I smoke all the time – long thin cigars, as many as I can smoke without being sick. I quite like that – filling myself all day long with nothing. There is no reality to the sustenance of a body which is headed towards obsolescence. The mind is the only reality. The loss of the brain is a far greater fear than the loss of sexuality. Much too much is made of the other thing.

'I don't listen to music while I work. The work itself is a kind of music. In the evenings I like to write music for recreation. At the moment I am doing a symphony for a suite of four songs by D.H. Lawrence and I'm writing an opera about Freud. If I feel a need for inspiration I read the OED. I've just written a very long book on language teaching. It is one of my great interests as I started my career as a phonetician.

'I am also engaged in writing a novel in verse, in *ottavia rima*, the form pioneered in Italy by Ariosto and later copied by Byron in *Don Juan*. The discipline is intense. I don't much like writing, although it's the only thing I can do. The critics say I have written far too much – Burgess baiting, my wife calls it. I don't think I'll ever write another novel. I'm getting old. I was baptized as a Catholic but abandoned religion when I was young and then went back to it out of fear and later out of interest. I now realize that what happens in the next life is completely irrelevant. Even if I do carry on in some form, it won't be me as I am now and all I can think of is the time I have wasted that will never come again.'

Anthony Burgess has written fifty-two books (thirty of them novels)

including the Booker Prize-winning *Earthly Powers*. His latest novel was *Mozart and the Wolf Gang*. His most recent publication was *A Mouthful of Air: Language, and Languages, Especially English*.

Sir Victor (V.S.) Pritchett

'I do think about death a bit,' Sir Victor Pritchett admits. 'I think, how inconvenient, I might be dead at the end of the year. I don't imagine there's any after-life. My father was a Christian Scientist. He believed that you went on just the same, but without your body. That seems to me rather a waste of time.'

He is ninety-two. Now and then, he muses, he catches himself out playing the role of an old gentleman: 'When I begin to work, I light up a pipe very confidently. It goes out almost at once. After an hour, I think, "Oh, God, where's my pipe?"'

In 1990 he was awarded the WH Smith Award for his most recent collection of short stories, *A Careless Widow*. This year, he says, he feels the start of the frightening process of slowing down. 'I have a number of exercise books in which I write down ideas for stories. I open them from time to time and find that they are absolutely useless. It is what is in my head now that interests me. I write three lines and then I come to a stop. At the moment there are several stories I would like to write but I can't force them. Every story has to be an adventure.

'I don't think I've ever helped a story along by falling back on the conventional phrase. Old age makes one ramble. Sometimes I get so dispirited I want to kick myself.'

In discussion of his favourite subject – the short story – he is wholly alert and assured. 'The tale begins at the moment of its enactment.' Over morning coffee in his sunny drawing-room with velvet sofas and embroidered cushions Sir Victor reveals the art of writing fiction. 'You do not think up a plot. You do not invent, you relate. The story is led by character. The character describes himself without knowing it.'

He wrote his first successful story, 'A Sense of Humour', when he was in his twenties and on holiday in Ireland – 'in a dreadful boring place called Enniskillen.' The story was based on an exact account of a meeting with an agricultural official there. 'I wrote it all the wrong way first of all. I thought up some sort of plot. After a year in which my effort kept coming back I realized that the life of the story was in the man's actual words. When I forgot myself and my activity and only thought of him and his exact speech and what his interests were, this showed me how to write. I had hit upon a way of writing that was just coming in, which employed a lot of dialogue to reveal a type of character with which the reader might be unfamiliar. This was the start of real speech in fiction, instead of traditional novelists' speech.'

This adherence to reality has, he confesses, involved him in some thin-ice skating. 'A lot of my stories relate to my own life. Then I have had the rather delicate task of translating it into fiction. Sometimes, when sufficiently excited by an incident, I have raced home to write it immediately.' He looks surprised by the suggestion that this practice might have brought about some resentments. 'I have frequently exploited a relationship for fiction but I've always transferred it to another scene,' he protests. 'Events past need a change of scene to bring them to life. I haven't so much written about my life as used incidents that touched on my life. Otherwise, I'd just be writing about myself. I think and hope the stories are apart from me. I've been very much a listener. I used to be good at listening to people's dodges of conversation.'

At the start of his tenth decade he still sets himself to work at nine-thirty every day. 'Writing's hard work and it's boring, but I like it.' Victor Pritchett has not bothered to get to grips with technology. 'I've got an assortment of rotting pens that have run out of ink. I type after an appalling three-fingered fashion, but all my manuscripts are done by hand. I have a room full of them. I sold a few early on. People used to come around to buy them but now I drive them away because I realized they were rather

diddling me,' he grins. 'I haven't disposed of a manuscript for a good many years.

'My hand-writing is awful but my wife understands it and she does my typing.' He blames his bad hand-writing on a schoolmaster called Bartlett who introduced a fashion for half-script writing to Camberwell Grammar School in 1910 but praises this teacher for opening up his imagination, as did his mother – 'a real racing cockney whose stories and use of language were very influential.'

Lately, he says, he finds himself thinking more and more about his father and accepting that he too was an unlikely inspiration. 'He was a very pious man. As a boy I used to be mad about the cheap schoolboy papers like *The Magnet*. Once, my father caught me reading one of these. He snatched it from me and tore it up. "You must read what's decent!" he said. He didn't know what was decent, but he assumed that I did. After that, I remember lying in bed at the age of twelve or thirteen, getting gripped by Shakespeare. As I grew up I made myself read in French and German, which was very difficult. For translating, you have to find the exact equivalent of the voice that's speaking. It was all a part of the search for clarity.'

Old age, he says, by turns makes him angry, amused and interested. 'I'm angry when I make serious mistakes or blunders. If I see something I've written that isn't right, I get furious and think, "What a fool I was."'

He is amused, suddenly, to think of himself as the focus of talk of old age and death. 'I'm frightfully healthy, but it's worth knowing death is there because it makes you more aware of life. I've been around a long time and I think I've learnt a thing or two about life. 'You've got to live it like mad!'

V.S. Pritchett is the most distinguished man of letters living today. A novelist, short-story writer, critic, travel writer, biographer and autobiographer, he was knighted in 1975 and is a member of both the American Academy of Arts and Letters and the Academy of Arts and Sciences. He recently received the Order of the Companions of Honour.

Firdaus Kanga

Firdaus Kanga is one of the few happy writers I have met. The 32-year-old Bombay-born novelist, travel writer and critic declares straight away that he likes writing 'better than anything in the world. I have had a little life but in writing you can use everything. Nothing is wasted.'

A tiny, suave figure in a racy motorized wheelchair, Kanga has been disabled from birth with brittle bone disease. A large part of his childhood was spent howling with pain as bones 'as thin as test tubes' crumbled when he attempted to walk. His illness has restricted his growth to that of an eight-year-old. 'Also, I am gay.' He converted this set of circumstances into a delightfully merry and funny first novel, *Trying to Grow*.

Kanga writes in bed. He works through the night, writing from midnight until three a.m. He has never used a typewriter. 'I don't know if I could sit up that long.' His handwritten exercise books are sent out to be typed. 'In India,' he reflects wistfully, 'you can have your typing done for twenty pence a page. Here it is two pounds a page.'

Coming to England has been a great release. 'In England I can be myself. In India the whole business of handicap is surrounded with pity and horror. A disabled person is either a legless beggar on a skateboard or else people assume you have done something unspeakable in a previous incarnation. Of course, homosexuality simply isn't mentioned at all. I remember fancying men from the age of four or five. I didn't know anything about homosexuality until I read articles in my mother's copy of *Woman's Own*. They always said, "This is a phase which will pass."'

Kanga spent the first nineteen years of his life in bed until the acquisition of a wheelchair. 'We had a tiny flat in Bombay. We lived comfortably but we couldn't afford property. There was no room for a wheelchair.' A house move in 1977 was accompanied by the liberating gift of his first set of wheels. 'I have had a tremendously privileged life,' he insists. 'First of all my family are Parsees, which means we were very liberal and did not grow up surrounded by gods. I was carried to the theatre and libraries. My family carried me across the road to a private teacher. When I was twelve, my father, who was a salesperson for Transworld Airlines, carried me around the world.'

He wrote his novel while living with his family in Bombay and spent two years looking for a literary agent in London. 'There was this completely ridiculous dream that I would go to live in Britain.' To the terror of his mother, an invitation arrived from a friend studying music in London. Equipped with a new motorized wheelchair, Kanga took on the whole of Britain, travelling for four months, taking notes and taping conversations. His irreverent English journey is recorded in a hilarious book, *Heaven on Wheels*.

He lives and works in a borrowed flat in West Hampstead, supporting himself, between books, with reviewing, and, 'thrill of thrills', has recently been granted a writer's visa, which will enable him to stay.

It is a precarious existence, but Kanga is not concerned. 'I do everything because I am terrified of everything,' he says.

Firdaus Kanga's two books, *Trying to Grow* and *Heaven on Wheels*, are available in paperback.

Beryl Bainbridge

Beryl Bainbridge always works in white cotton gloves. 'I have stacks of them – 75p a pair in Boots. It's to keep the nicotine off my fingers.' Her tall terraced house in Camden Town is tiered into an assortment of studies. 'I start off in the kitchen, working with pen and paper on the kitchen table, then I move up to my typewriter on the first floor and later on I go to the word processor which is at the top of the house. The top room is a tip, full of cig ash and bits of paper. I keep the word processor there out of sight, like the telly, because it is so ugly.'

Bainbridge begins each novel in the kitchen with 'a nice new hardbacked notebook. Somehow it ends up full of shopping lists or bits get torn off it to light the gas stove. When I am really at work I use white paper in A4 size and I always use a black drawing pen with a very fine nib. The vital accessories to my work are my reference books, such as the complete Shakespeare and a prayer book, and a large black refuse bin.

'When I am finished with my notes in the kitchen I carry them up to the typewriter and after they have been typed up I move to the top floor with both notes and typescripts and edit the two on to the word processor. I never throw anything out until a novel is completely finished. It all goes into my bin. This is completely practical. It saves the anxiety of discovering that an earlier version was better than a final one, but now it's lost, and it means that when the book is finished, I can simply dump the surplus matter out for the bin men in one go.

'I used to work from eight in the evening until three in the morning when the children were small because I could only write

when they were in bed. Now I get up at 6 a.m. I have an appalling breakfast – a cup of hot water with gelatin in it, because I'm trying to grow my fingernails. It makes me feel so horrible I can't even manage a cup of tea after that. I always plan on something eggy later on but after the first five fags my appetite's gone.

'While I am working I don't dress or wash or anything. It's not a normal sort of life at all. One day recently, I thought, "this is ridiculous," so I tucked my nightie into my boots, put on an overcoat, went out and walked round and round the park like mad. It made me feel very ill indeed.'

It was a relief to learn that Beryl Bainbridge finally gets round to food at around 5.30 in the evening. 'I boil up a lot of potatoes and have them with something really dreadful, like a sausage. Eating always makes me tired so then I lie down for a bit. When I get up I watch *Coronation Street* on the telly and after that I go upstairs and do some typing. At this point I am not so much finishing off the day's work as starting work for the following day.

'When I go to bed I read out aloud over and over what I have written so far – sometimes as much as 50 pages. If you know something's not quite right and you force yourself to listen to it, sooner or later the right phrase comes into your head.

'When I had a house full of children I used to think it would be wonderful to have the place to myself and all the peace I needed to write. Now I realize that it is so much easier to deal with the frustrations of everyday life than to have to face oneself all day long. Sometimes I think of getting a job and then sneaking home in the evenings to write. I live like a recluse. You can't share a bed with anyone if you're going to read aloud all night. I avoid quarrels because they make me miserable and then I can't work, so it means that vital issues in relationships never get confronted. Most of the time I wonder what it's all for. It's a mug's game. It's no way for a normal person to live.'

Beryl Bainbridge has written thirteen novels and a number of stage and

screenplays. She has been three times short-listed for the Booker Prize and was a winner of the *Guardian* Fiction Prize with *The Bottle Factory Outing*. Her most recent novel, *The Birthday Boys*, is published by Duckworth.

BY THE SAME AUTHOR

Home Rule

Growing up in the Dublin of the 1890s is far from easy for Daisy Devlin. Tormented by the whims of her brothers and sisters, her distant melodramatic mother and the adoring father with whom she shares a guilty secret, Daisy longs to be rescued from her troubles. Escaping to a convent at the age of seventeen, she violently resists the encroachment of womanhood until the day she meets Cecil Cantwell, the blond, blue-eyed soldier who promises to transform her destiny . . .

and its sequel

Holy Pictures

In the Dublin of 1925 the holy scriptures are about to be superseded by moving pictures. To fourteen-year-old Nan the cinema appears as a miraculous rescue from the confines of her Catholic upbringing. But growing up into a world of immoral, unreliable adults is not easy, and the last year of Nan's childhood moves from the burlesque to the tragic . . .

Black Baby

On the day of her First Communion, Alice had paid the nuns half a crown to adopt a black baby from the mission in Africa. Mysteriously, the longed-for baby never arrived . . .

Fifty years on, Dinah turns up on Alice's doorstep. Unnervingly black, bawdy and splendid, her leather skirt curving like an iron cooking pot, her red high heels clicking, Dinah holds Dublin in the palm of her hand. And for Alice, she spells the beginning of dreams come almost true.

and

Concerning Virgins

PENGUIN BOOKS

Published by the Penguin Group
Penguin Books Ltd, 27 Wrights Lane, London w8 5tz, England
Penguin Books USA Inc., 375 Hudson Street, New York, New York 10014, USA
Penguin Books Australia Ltd, Ringwood, Victoria, Australia
Penguin Books Canada Ltd, 10 Alcorn Avenue, Toronto, Ontario, Canada m4v 3b2
Penguin Books (NZ) Ltd, 182–190 Wairau Road, Auckland 10, New Zealand

Penguin Books Ltd, Registered Offices: Harmondsworth, Middlesex, England

First published 1993
1 3 5 7 9 10 8 6 4 2

Filmset in 10/13 pt Monophoto Sabon
Typeset by Datix International Limited, Bungay, Suffolk
Printed in England by Clays Ltd, St Ives plc

THE AGONY
AND
THE EGO

The Art and Strategy of Fiction Writing Explored

Clare Boylan

PENGUIN BOOKS

RSAC S

THE AGONY AND THE EGO

Clare Boylan was born and grew up in Dublin, which is the setting for three of her novels. An award-winning journalist, she turned to fiction, enjoying widespread success with her short stories, which have been adapted into films and published in many countries as well as in her collections *A Nail on the Head* and *Concerning Virgins*. After a career that has included playwriting, radio and television broadcasting, close-harmony singing, editing two magazines, bookselling and cutting the heads off cabbages in the back room of a grocery shop, she now confines herself to short and long fiction, cats, literary criticism and some journalism. Penguin also publish her novels *Last Resorts*, *Black Baby*, *Home Rule*, and its sequel *Holy Pictures*.

Clare Boylan lives in Wicklow with her journalist husband, and a cat and a dog, Gertie and Bertie.

D1126912